Praise for *Lead with Heart and Leave a Legacy*

"Tricia Manning's Lead with Heart and Leave a Legacy *heralds the change that is fast approaching corporate cultures. We are long past the time when results are what define a successful leader. Results plus presence plus heart are now required. Manning gives you a deeply personal view into her journey, leaving the reader with powerful insights and practical advice on how you, too, can find your way to leading with heart."*

—**Ingrid Lindberg**, *CEO of Chief Customer and Cofounder of aubreyAsks*

"Tricia does an excellent job telling her story and the lessons she learned along her twenty-five-year journey that helped mold her into being a caring leader (not a boss). Readers will be able to relate to, and I think appreciate much more, how she learned to be a leader, why it should be important to them, and the benefit real leaders provide their companies. This is a book that every leader should read and keep close to their heart, whether they are just starting out or are committed to constantly getting better by speaking less and listening and learning more."

—**Roy Simrell**, *CEO, Prometric*

"I had the pleasure of serving with Tricia on an executive leadership team during a challenging time at our company. I watched her come onto a team faced with very tough choices and bring humanity, empathy, and, importantly, the business case for never losing sight of the criticality of the human side of leadership. I learned from watching Tricia influence decisions, deliver results, and grow and keep high-performing teams that my notion of what successful leadership meant was missing a focus on the 'heart' needed to elevate a leader from effective to inspirational. I now draw daily off of Tricia's actions and counsel in leading my teams, and I and my teams are all the better for it. I am thrilled that she has chosen to write this book to share her special wisdom with other leaders so many can benefit from her leadership legacy."

—**Tamara L. Meyer**, *Vice President, Assistant General Counsel, WellCare Health Plans*

"Tricia and I were peers climbing the corporate ladder at the same time, and I was fortunate to work with her as a business partner for twenty-two years. I always admired Tricia's leadership style. While ascending to her role as an executive leader, she continued to care deeply for her teams and was an active listener who led her teams to take a collaborative approach to problem-solving. She was fair, confident, and calm under pressure. With this book, Tricia maintains her authentic voice while she shares her experiences, perspective, and passion to bring valued insight to help those in search of career guidance during times of transition and transformation."

—**Jennifer Burke**, *Former President, Catalina; Current Industry Executive for Microsoft Corporation*

"*Every day there are countless opportunities to be intentional in how you lead and to create new possibility and potential for yourself and your teams.*

A good leadership book causes one to pause and reflect. In Lead with Heart and Leave a Legacy, *Tricia Manning shares powerful leadership lessons and explores the importance of leading intentionally with actionable insights, such as listening more than talking and collaborating with your team. The anecdotes shared in the book are not hyperbolic feel-good tales of leadership—they are insightful and full of aha moments that made me reflect and rethink my leadership approach.*

If you are an experienced leader who wants a fresh perspective on how to continue to operate at your best and to help others be their very best and/or you are at a place in your life where it's time to reevaluate your life and pivot, this book is for you."

—**Renée Baker**, *Head of Advisor Inclusion Networks, Raymond James*

"*I had the pleasure of working alongside Tricia for eighteen of my twenty-two years at Catalina. Tricia's brand of leadership was both empowering and inspirational. This proved to be a powerful combination that drove business results and developed team members to be the best they could be. The beauty was in the 'and!'*"

—**Debbie Booth**, *Retired EVP, Global Operations and Chief Performance Excellence Officer, Catalina*

"Authentic, inspiring, empowering, brave—this is Tricia Manning. I know this firsthand from my more than ten years as an executive member of her leadership team. It is a rare and unique opportunity to be led by someone with Tricia's heart and unparalleled belief that when you take care of the people, when you encourage and enable them to be the best version of themselves, they will, in turn, take care of the business, the clients, and each other. It is from that belief that Tricia developed her leadership style and values. Her unwavering commitment to be her true authentic self created a culture of transparency, trust, and confidence to lead with heart. Not only did Tricia leave a legacy at Catalina, but that legacy continues to spread through the executive leadership coaching she is doing today. To have the opportunity to be coached and mentored by Tricia is a gift that will have immeasurable impact on the people and businesses she serves."

—**Rose Buggé**, *Certified Business and Executive Coach, Business Owner, ActionCOACH*

LEAD WITH

heart

& LEAVE A

legacy

Be Intentional!

Nicie Manning

TRICIA MANNING

LEAD WITH

heart

& LEAVE A

legacy

LEARN TO BE

intentional

IN HOW YOU LEAD

Advantage.

Published by Advantage, Charleston, South Carolina.
Member of Advantage Media Group.

ADVANTAGE is a registered trademark, and the Advantage colophon is a trademark of Advantage Media Group, Inc.

Printed in the United States of America.

10 9 8 7 6 5 4 3 2 1

ISBN: 978-1-64225-143-2
LCCN: 2019913004

Book design by Megan Elger.

This publication is designed to provide accurate and authoritative information in regard to the subject matter covered. It is sold with the understanding that the publisher is not engaged in rendering legal, accounting, or other professional services. If legal advice or other expert assistance is required, the services of a competent professional person should be sought.

Advantage Media Group is proud to be a part of the Tree Neutral® program. Tree Neutral offsets the number of trees consumed in the production and printing of this book by taking proactive steps such as planting trees in direct proportion to the number of trees used to print books. To learn more about Tree Neutral, please visit **www.treeneutral.com**.

Advantage Media Group is a publisher of business, self-improvement, and professional development books and online learning. We help entrepreneurs, business leaders, and professionals share their Stories, Passion, and Knowledge to help others Learn & Grow. Do you have a manuscript or book idea that you would like us to consider for publishing? Please visit **advantagefamily.com** or call **1.866.775.1696**.

This book is dedicated to all the leaders, entrepreneurs, and business professionals who are committed to personal and professional growth—those people who aspire to be their best selves and make a positive and lasting impact on those they serve along the way.

CONTENTS

ACKNOWLEDGMENTS

To my mom and my role model, for what it looks like to be a strong, independent, and capable woman. Life wasn't as expected, and you faced adversity with a quiet strength that taught me resiliency, responsibility, and most importantly compassion. You have given me so many gifts, with the most precious being the ability to see the best in all situations and in all people. Your unconditional love and selfless support for others enables possibility and has greatly influenced the purpose in my work today.

To my husband, who loves me unconditionally and is my biggest fan. There was a greater plan at work when you came into my life, and I will never forget the day I knew I could get through anything with you by my side. I will forever be grateful for your encouragement to tell my story and for the love and joy you and your children bring to my life every single day.

To my son, who makes me so proud. You are kind and compassionate and intuitive beyond measure. Your greatest gift is your heart, and while you are still maneuvering this world and your place in it, there will be a time when you impact the lives of many and come to recognize your special gift to this world.

To all the women whom I admire and who have supported me in my journey. I am blessed with friendships that run deep and authentic connections that have come into my life for a reason and will forever leave their mark on my heart. These relationships represent the beauty and the power that can exist when we support one another without judgment.

HOW TO SEE POSSIBILITIES IN YOURSELF AND OTHERS

Leading with heart involves connecting with people, identifying what motivates and inspires them, and helping them see possibility in themselves that they didn't know existed. Leading with heart is one way to leave a lasting impact on the people around you to leave a legacy.

As a leader, my goal has always been to support others and create opportunity for everyone to feel successful. I draw energy and excitement from lifting others up. Over the years, I have maintained a fundamental belief that leaders are directly responsible for helping others to find their right fit: meaningful and valuable work for them personally that provides an opportunity for them to develop their personal best self.

When an employee is their best self at work, the company gets the best outcome.

So how do you, as a leader, extract this possibility and potential in those you lead?

When an employee is their best self at work, the company gets the best outcome.

In this book you will find ways to be a highly engaged leader and understand what inspires, motivates, and connects people individually. You will have the knowledge to find the sweet spot where you operate at your best and understand more clearly the role you play in helping others do their best work.

You will recognize what it means to lead with heart and understand that, by being intentional in *how* you lead, you can create a lasting legacy.

The leadership lessons I share have transcended my work as a coach. I am committed to supporting smart business leaders who are managing it all—personally and professionally—and to help them elevate their leadership skills and develop new possibilities for themselves.

One of the most requested areas of focus with the majority of my coaching clients has to do with authentic leadership. I am often asked, How do I bring my best self to my work? Can you help me find ways to remain my authentic, unique self as I develop my career?

I actually love these questions, and I will share a little about my story to explain why.

I had a long and successful career at the same company for twenty-five years. I started in an entry-level position and worked my way up to an executive vice president position in a global role reporting directly to the CEO. Like many others today, my company was going through a significant digital transformation. There was a lot of change—in leadership, strategy, product offerings, and go-to-market strategy—and I found it to be my role, my responsibility as someone who had been with the organization for so long and who had worked with the original founders in the early days, to intentionally lead the organization through this very large change. I made it my mission to take what was so special and unique about the history, tradition, and culture of this amazing organization and bring it forward into our new world. It was hard work. Day after day, I was faced with the challenge of remaining true to my authentic self while I influenced new leadership, drove a new strategy, molded a new culture, and ultimately did what I thought was the right thing for over 1,200 employees relying on me.

I was committed to the work—in my heart and my head.

Then everything changed. It was late 2016 when I went for an executive physical and received the news that I had two significant health issues. Within thirty days of this news—and after many more tests, doctor visits, and decisions—I was on the operating table at forty-four years old, having open-heart surgery. While I would recover and be perfectly healthy on the other side of it all, it was a life-changing experience. It forced me to rethink my priorities and gain clarity into what I wanted to be doing with the rest of my life. It wasn't long after I recovered and went back to work that I made the decision to wind down my twenty-five-year career and start a new chapter.

It was a health scare that made me explore more deeply my own potential and focus on two very important questions:

Who do I want to be every day when I wake up?

How do I want to contribute?

This was the greatest decision point in my career. My personal health scare started me on my journey to live my best life. I knew this was my chance to own the journey, find my purpose, and do the self-exploration necessary to be successful in my next endeavor as a coach.

During this time of self-reflection, I was able to step back and take an objective look at the impact I'd had as a leader. People kept using the word *legacy* to describe my leadership, but it wasn't just about me personally. It was also what I represented in my role as a leader: a senior executive who started in an entry-level position with a front-row seat to the early days of the company, a consistent voice over the years committed to getting the teams rallied around the organization's goals, and a relatable leader who showed interest in others and worked hard to learn what motivated them. This was what it was all about.

To get here required a sustained belief in myself, and now life was trying to tell me something and steer me in a new direction. I am glad I decided to listen.

I am now on my new path, but I am not done learning. I may be one year, five years, or maybe only five minutes ahead of you down this road. It is okay that I am continuing to figure it out. I love that I am constantly learning and experiencing new lessons every day. Learning opportunities are everywhere!

In this book I bring these learnings—my own aha moments—and the insights from those inspirational leaders I have sought out, listened to, and even led or coached over the years. I am fortunate to have had a sandbox, a trusted and safe environment, to apply the lessons over the years. I have figured out what works for me personally. In sharing these lessons, I am giving you the opportunity to apply them to your own work and accelerate your own leadership possibilities while being true to your values, beliefs, and style.

Possibilities for greatness are in our own reach, and we have a choice each day in how we approach our work. Every day there are countless opportunities to be intentional in *how* you lead and to create new possibilities and potential for yourself and your teams.

My goal for the next phase of my life is to teach people how to lead with heart, make a lasting impact, and leave a legacy everywhere they go. In this book you'll hear even more about my story and how this significant health scare gave me clarity and inspired me to help others lead with heart. I will help you discover the following:

> *Every day there are countless opportunities to be intentional in how you lead and to create new possibilities and potential for yourself and your teams.*

- what it means to lead with heart,

- how to be the voice for your people,

- how to capture your own voice,

- how to be a continuous learner,

- how to redefine success, and

- how to know when it's time to start your own next chapter.

Whether you're a growth-minded leader looking for ways to accelerate success or you're looking to begin a new chapter in your life, this book will show you how to lead with heart and leave a legacy wherever you go.

Let's get started.

CHAPTER 1

LEADING WITH HEART

The fact that I was born in New Jersey may conjure up all sorts of images, thoughts, and questions, but the truth is my parents met in high school and got married there shortly after. My younger brother and I enjoyed regular family trips to Florida, where my grandparents lived after retiring, and after years of racking up endless doctor bills from being sick during the winter months, my parents decided to move all of us to Florida's warmer climate permanently. My father didn't want to make the move because his parents were still living in New Jersey and he was making good money as an engineer. Though he wasn't excited about moving to Florida, he did it anyway to please my mother.

I was only five years old when my father started to have some health issues, but no one could figure out what was wrong. He went to see all sorts of specialists and spent time in hospitals all over Florida before finally being diagnosed with multiple sclerosis. By the time I was twelve, he could no longer work. That changed our lives considerably, especially our family dynamic. Though my mom had an education degree, she was only working as a part-time librarian at the local elementary school my brother and I attended. The Americans with Disabilities Act did not work in my dad's favor, and my mom was forced to take on the role of caregiver for him while she supported our family, entering the full-time working world as a high-school math teacher.

The most important model for me, and the person who had the most impact on my style of leadership, was my mom. From an early age, I viewed my mom as a very strong, resilient woman who made a 180-degree turn in her life with grace and strength to keep our family going. It was hard enough dealing with our new family dynamic because my father couldn't work and needed full-time care. Since he was a strong-minded individual, my dad was a big influence in my life as he lived vicariously through me. He wanted me to achieve success in life, which he defined as having money, and that was something instilled inside of me as I started working at age thirteen as a babysitter.

Growing up, our dinner table conversations always included the question, How much money did you make today? These conversations had a huge impact on me because I have subconsciously put expectations on myself about what success looks like based on what my dad taught me. My mom, on the other hand, was very focused on making sure my brother and I had everything we needed and didn't miss a beat when it came time to go to college.

LEAVING FOR COLLEGE

It didn't feel right leaving my parents to go off to college while my mom still had my dad to take care of, but they were both supportive of me continuing my education. I always knew I wanted to go away to school even though I wasn't exactly clear about what I wanted to do. My dad encouraged professions that made a lot of money; however, that created a lot of anxiety in me because I always pictured myself owning my own business. When I started out exploring colleges, like so many other young adults, I had no idea what was out there, much less which profession to choose.

Fortunately, during high school, I got a part-time job through a recommendation from a girlfriend who worked at a local college for their continuing education program. They hosted leadership development programs for business executives from around the world who would fly in and spend a week at the college to meet with coaches and leadership development professionals. The course involved taking all sorts of tests, such as the Myers–Briggs Type Indicator (MBTI), the Fundamental Interpersonal Relations Orientation-Behavior (FIRO-B) test, 360s, and so on, allowing executives to learn about themselves and their personal leadership styles. I worked in that program, and my role was to put all the packets and training materials together. I could see all these incredible resources and tools that the program offered and was fascinated with how these executives were assessed.

I was so curious about the program that I asked if could sit in on the sessions. Since a lot of the sessions were recorded, I asked if I could man the camera and videotape the sessions to learn more about this investment around leadership and self-discovery. I soon realized how powerful it was for some of these executives, who would sometimes break down crying through the very personal and intense process.

Grown men and women were taking a hard look in the mirror to really understand how they were behaving and where they had gaps in their leadership abilities. They received feedback from their employees and self-assessments of their style of leadership in order to realize they had some blind spots that they weren't aware of. They used the tools they were given to realize how their approach could be the cause of various challenges on their teams. The fact that the company they worked for wanted to invest in them and support them in this self-discovery and ultimately the process of their behavior change was incredible. This was a defining moment for me at a young age. I had new awareness of the importance of leadership and got to see firsthand how the focus on leadership behaviors and self-reflection, coupled with a strong coach, could have such a positive and significant impact on an accomplished professional.

This was my early definition of leadership development: provide the resources and support needed for the leader to get feedback, facilitate a process of self-discovery, and intentionally create a plan to improve. They leave the program knowing themselves better, seeking self-improvement, changing how they lead, and doing it with intention. This experience was a gift for me. What I didn't learn until later was that not all leaders would take the time and not all companies would make the investment for this professional development.

I entered college at Florida State and lived on campus, where I was far enough from home but not too far if I needed to get home quickly. It was my early exposure to human behavior and relationship dynamics that sparked my interest in psychology, but I gave into the pressures from my father to make money and achieve success as he defined it. After a few classes in accounting, which I didn't like, I decided to finish with a degree in finance. Like most students when they graduate from college, I was ready to be done with school and get out in the real world to apply what I learned. Immediately after graduation, I went home and started looking for a job. My mom showed me an ad in the paper with big, bold letters asking, Do you want to relocate to sunny California for the summer?

START-UP

Intrigued, I applied and luckily got the job. It turned out to be a fast-growing start-up marketing company that was founded by five friends in California who decided to move the headquarters to Florida. My training was held in California before I headed back to Florida to begin my entry-level position, but I was so intrigued by the entrepreneurial spirit of this company and how they treated the California employees with respect and care when it came time to move to Florida. They turned out to be a pioneer in the marketing industry, offering an electronic marketing system that delivered coupons and promotional messages targeted to consumers based on what they purchased at the grocery store. Reaching more than 130 million shoppers, they had a mission to help families save money on food, diapers, and general grocery items.

There was so much to learn, and it wasn't long before I had more exposure to executives and was being put on assignments that helped progress my career into leadership. Now I had people who were reporting to me, which gave me hands-on experience as to what it meant to be a leader. Through my experience, I observed both

Through my experience, I observed both good and bad leadership and knew the difference between a boss and a leader. My goal was to be a leader.

good and bad leadership and knew the difference between a boss and a leader. My goal was to be a leader.

There was so much inspiration around me, and I started to home in on the fact that I could make a unique difference by showing care and concern for the people as well as the business. I wanted to support others and create opportunities for them to be and feel successful. As a leader, my goal was to engage with them, motivate them, and lift them up, and soon I had a reputation for always making people feel better—inspired and energized—after we had a conversation. Since I had felt this exact way coming into the company, I wanted everyone who came to see me to feel that way too. When I would interview potential candidates or meet new employees for the first time, it was never hard to answer the question, What has kept you here so long?

My reply was always the same: "I always feel like I am making a difference. It is like a sandbox that allows me to try different things and focus on what I am good at—coaching and mentoring people."

It was a great experience. The things I've learned over the past twenty-five years have led me to figure out a way to lead with the heart and leave a lasting impact on the people I have led. I've done this by valuing personal connections with others, listening to and understanding their needs, and finding a common ground to move forward. Throughout my career, I have observed the qualities of both effective and ineffective leaders—those who had a memorable way of bringing out the best in people and those who had the best intentions but who just couldn't get results. It was these experiences that started me on my journey to help others.

What do you want to be known for? Do you want to leave a legacy behind? Let this book take you on a journey of leading with heart that will be rewarding, worthwhile, and gratifying in so many ways. Let's keep going.

CHAPTER 2

A QUARTER-CENTURY CAREER BEGINS

When I began my entry-level position at Catalina, I was so grateful to join such an exciting new company that promised rapid growth in the marketing and promotions industry. Initially, my duties involved writing the text that appeared on the coupons printed at grocery store checkout lanes. Let me explain: going back thirty-five-plus years, when the company was founded, they built a proprietary network with retailers. One by one they went to companies such as Kroger, Winn-Dixie, Food Lion, and Safeway to convince them to allow Catalina to connect to the retailer's point of sale system. They monitored transaction data in every lane in every one of those stores.

Their approach involved creating a triangular relationship among the consumer packaged goods (CPG) manufacturers, grocery retailers, and Catalina. Catalina would contract with brands such as Pampers, Kleenex, Brawny, Betty Crocker, and so on to issue promotional campaigns to millions of shoppers. The beauty of this solution is that Catalina brought this brand content to those retailers, allowing them to communicate directly with their customers and create loyalty to their retail chain. Retailers were very interested in what Catalina could bring to them.

Living in Southern California before making the transition to St. Petersburg, Florida, allowed me to work directly with the founders. It was thrilling as well as fascinating watching how both the senior leaders and founders made decisions with such care and concern for all involved during their rapid growth. They didn't just make business decisions but also people decisions because not all California employees were willing to move their families to Florida, and as a result, they would be out of a job. Catalina's leadership provided weekly communication to all employees on the progress of the relocation and were personally invested in helping each of these employees find their next opportunity before the company finalized the move.

This was the culture they created for their organization, something I supported from the very beginning. The company could reach and achieve its goals in a way that would bring other people along and create a positive environment during such a time of change. It was a differentiator for any company. I would stay with Catalina for twenty-five years, working my way up from the entry level to the C-suite and bringing these early lessons and observations with me along the way.

LEADERSHIP STYLES

I dealt with many people at my company who were in positions of leadership over the years; most of them were men, but there were several women as well. Focusing on the leadership styles of the women and thinking about what it was that made them someone I would either like to emulate or not was truly impactful on me. Watching everyone from internal leaders to external customers allowed me to develop the ability to see how a situation could become derailed quickly. It became clear to me how behaviors during a crisis could negatively affect the outcome when a leader showed anger and placed blame. Even an organizational win could be a challenge for a leader who takes all the credit and doesn't recognize the efforts of the collective team.

While I had exposure to both positive and negative scenarios and worked directly with different types of leaders, the leader who gave me my first taste of "Wow, I can do anything!" was a leader who actually connected with and engaged my heart. She cared about me and what I had going on—not just at work but at home too. She spent time explaining why we were doing something, not taking a directive approach but rather a collaborative one. She respected my opinion, set high expectations, and then would immediately ask, What do you need to make that happen? It was a level of connection that inspired excellence, and I wanted to make her proud.

Despite this woman's ability to lead and develop a team of people to perform, I noticed that she was not perceived as very impactful in her communications, and she didn't appear to be in succession for a senior-level role. I found this perplexing and wondered why another woman who was much more aggressive in her communication and whom not many people were clamoring to work for would have a different level of respect among her peers. What was it about her leadership style that made her difficult to work for yet highly respected and seen as someone who was headed up the corporate ladder? Would it be possible to combine the two styles and come up with an approach that would enable someone to succeed while remaining true to themselves?

Neither of these leadership styles were an exact fit for me, so it became my mission to move up in the organization and be perceived as a key contributor and player at the senior levels but do so with care, concern, and authenticity. The direct effect a manager could have on an employee's personal decision to stay or leave a company was something I wanted to fully understand. I had seen those leaders who, on paper, accomplished the job at hand but were the cause of good people walking out the door. Growing a business and growing a career while staying authentic to who you are is an art, and that is when I started to really focus on being intentional in my *how*: how I showed up every day, how I engaged others, how I chose to lead. Soon people began responding to this style of leadership.

To do this, I needed to be a highly engaged leader, harness the abilities of my team, set clear goals and high expectations, and engage productive employees while keeping in mind the how.

How would I bring others along? Through good communication and collaboration. How would I give feedback? In a truthful yet compassionate way. How would I elicit high performance? By recognizing effort and caring about small wins. Over the years, I was able to hone those skills of having a strong presence and being mindfully present and drew my energy from the development and coaching of people.

Over time, my leadership style was recognized more broadly, and the impact it had across the organization was more apparent. I became a confidant to many people across the organization, taking an interest in their challenges and accomplishments. This was an opportunity to coach, develop, and strategically champion the important work that was going on within my direct team. These efforts led to a term that became known throughout the company as *cross-pollination*. We started to see people from different departments transfer in to learn new skills and contribute in new ways. Likewise, I was creating a coaching culture within my organization that encouraged movement to other parts of the organization. In short order, this was improving connections and engagement across the company.

EMBRACING DIVERSITY

Time marched on and organizational goals became more complicated and required multiple departments working together. Success was directly tied to my team's ability to influence priorities across the organization. My team now consisted of people I'd worked with for years and those newer to the company. We valued our diversity and differing points of view tremendously. This was a global team with leaders in Italy, Germany, France, and Japan.

Although it was a diverse team, the expectations set around leadership behaviors were nonnegotiable. I had modeled the behaviors of open lines of communication, encouraged learning, and facilitated connections, enabling my employees to become versed in building bridges and relationships with other teams to get things done. They were proud of what they accomplished and called themselves the GSD (Get Sh*t Done) team. This was a new level of accountability and an approach that would drive results. They took the time to listen, ask questions, and understand differing points of view, which gave other team members a supportive environment to take measured risks and own solutions. They consistently engaged with others in this way, creating a vested interest in working through problems.

I was proud of my team for being willing to influence positive outcomes across the organization by doing the heavy lifting but not taking the credit. We were all on the same team with a common goal of organizational and customer success, and it was happening exponentially through the people. You're going after a common goal, you're working together, you're supporting one another. Who wouldn't thrive in that kind of environment? The focus I placed on being visible and making connections was paying off, and I was inspired by the way they responded to this leadership style. It was my intention in how I led that allowed for development, growth, and the creation of opportunities for them to do their best work. It was through heart.

We were all on the same team with a common goal of organizational and customer success, and it was happening exponentially through the people.

MY PERSONAL LEADERSHIP STYLE

As my career progressed while I was implementing my own personal leadership approach, I was perceived as a strong leader with a reputation for driving returns in the business and in the people. I remained consistent and true to myself in how I ran the business and how I led the team. Although I didn't realize it at the time, I was using an actual formula for success that worked quite well.

Develop a leadership presence + be mindfully present + demonstrate care and concern for people. Unfortunately, most leaders only focus on part of the equation, but it's essential to put the entire formula into motion, beginning with presence.

Presence is one of the least developed skills and is a minimum requirement for any leader to grow their career. To become a great leader, you must have presence when you

- walk into a room,

- speak to a large group, and

- make a critical business decision.

Going hand in hand with presence is the important quality of being present. Not all leaders have mastered this talent, but most agree that it is a requirement to maneuver through the complications of a successful business in today's world. A senior leader must be in the moment to do the following:

- solve customer problems,

- respond to increasing shareholder expectations, and

- address competitive threats peering around the corner.

Finally, it is essential that you show concern for your people. Unfortunately, this is often the weakest link in the formula, but it just might be the most important. Most leaders have yet to drop the traditional leadership belief that showing emotion, care, and concern makes them appear weak. This couldn't be further from the truth! Demonstrating an interest and getting to know your employees personally and what touches their heart will have a tremendous impact on their engagement and performance.

We will cover more detail around what this can look like and ways you can put this formula to work later in the book.

BEING HEARD

As I mentioned, most leaders are weak in showing care for their people. How is this done? At work I was perceived as a good leader for being results oriented and focused on people development. However, one of the biggest reasons I stood out among my group and a key to my success in leading with heart was because I was the only one *not* talking. Yes, not talking. To truly understand what inspires, motivates, and connects people individually, you have to listen. Speak less and listen more.

To truly understand what inspires, motivates, and connects people individually, you have to listen. Speak less and listen more.

This was part of my own leadership style, and it was something I coached others to practice. Listening more and speaking less was foundational to being respected, building trust, and improving engagement. It wasn't the most widely leveraged strength among my peers, and I quickly saw that the higher up in the organization I went, the less listening and the more talking went on. Over the years, other leaders said, "You need to talk more. You need to make your opinion known." I even had leaders that would keep track of the number of times I spoke in a meeting! I experienced this a lot over the years but held true to my belief that it was not about me, my ego, and being heard; it was about saying the most impactful thing at the right time.

One of the most important lessons I learned was that people are more committed and engaged when they feel heard. When you are in a situation and really listening to someone, you can be significantly impactful by clarifying what you heard to help someone express their point of view or support their thoughts. Putting an exclamation point on what they're trying to say, really listening and demonstrating that you've heard what someone says, goes a long way in building relationships, credibility, and engagement.

During my time with the company, due to the changes in technology, information sharing, and customer expectations, everything began moving very fast. So many leaders are facing this exact challenge, and there is no time for consensus building to get to a decision. While this is true, you can't afford not to take the time to collaborate. Collaborating with your people—bringing them into decisions both large and small about changes that impact them directly—is an important way to help them feel heard. I anticipated reactions and would check in with my people, ask questions, and encourage discussion. Many leaders didn't have the patience or desire to engage with their teams in this way, but the investment of time early on helped to expedite the outcome. Collaboration was a way to create commitment to a goal and show them how they had a direct hand in the successful outcome in the end.

Over the years, the teams I led played a critical role in the company even though their work was mostly behind the scenes and not considered very sexy, unlike the work the sales and customer teams they supported did. However, at the end of the day, they were strategically executing the business with care and concern. My team became known for how they were accomplishing the work, and they started to take a more active role in coming to decisions with customers and the business itself. It began a shift.

New leaders and consultants would come into the organization and would often say, "Well, operations is the only group that's not messed up" or "Tricia and her leadership team are acknowledged as the group to model." All this was very humbling to me, but at the same time, my ideas about the best ways to lead were being affirmed. The system worked, and after being at the company for twenty-two years, I was promoted to the C-suite.

CHAPTER 3

THE CULTURE CARRIER

In a digital world, there is no future for a company that isn't committed to change, and I found myself in the executive vice president position at a critical point for the organization. There was a lot at stake, and it was now make-or-break time. Adding to the normal pressure of being responsible for helping the company pivot to digital, the present CEO was not thrilled with me taking the executive vice president seat. He believed that it was better to bring in new talent to facilitate the transformation, and so there were several organizational design changes under his leadership. We had a new CFO, CMO, and CPO—there were so many new C people coming in. His perspective was that the organization needed new thinking while the digital transformation was going on and that any shift could only be successful by bringing in new talent. It did not go as planned.

On a weekly basis, I braced myself for the inevitable question from one of my peers down the hall. "Can I give you some feedback?"

"Sure thing," I'd reply, all the while knowing what was coming with no choice but to listen.

"I was in a meeting today and met one of your employees. She has been here forever, and I don't really understand what she does. We can't make a digital transformation if we aren't willing to replace legacy thinking with new talent."

How was I supposed to deal with this way of thinking? Here I was leading the team responsible for executing a multimillion-dollar business built over the last thirty years on complex, proprietary systems. It was a team that would be responsible for maintaining quality and customer satisfaction during the transition, a team made up of knowledgeable, dedicated employees. It was these people, as well as many other employees across the organization, who would be the key to a successful transformation. Tapping into their commitment and connection to the company's culture and their desire to bring forward what made this company so great was an asset, not a liability. Why couldn't the new executives see this?

Tapping into their commitment and connection to the company's culture and their desire to bring forward what made this company so great was an asset, not a liability.

NEW THINKING

Respecting and understanding the importance of augmenting new thinking and experiences on a team, it was clear that, as executives, we were a long way from being aligned in our thinking and coming together to present ourselves as *one* team. We couldn't ignore the founders and the culture of care that was modeled from the early days. In the past we had always welcomed new people and diverse thinking, but no matter what needed to be done to transform, it was essential to keep the company culture top of mind.

With all these new players at the table, there were many different interpretations of how to handle this challenge, but the good news was that there was recognition from the top down that a digital transformation like this was going to be a large effort. Initially, I could see why each of these executives was selected for their role. Their ideas were innovative, and their intentions were good, so the recognizable stages of forming, storming, norming, and performing began.

There were early signs of progress that I could embrace, but it was like low-hanging fruit for a business that was behind in offering digital solutions in the marketplace. While a few new ideas about our products and our pricing model provided a glimpse into where we were going with this transformation, the bigger systemic change was slow to come, and the pressure was on. Each leader had their own paradigm and was approaching each new challenge and decision with blinders on. We weren't working together as a team, and after many months, we were still forming and storming with no real signs of norming or performing.

THE BEGINNING OF THE END

The lack of progress against the company strategy led to a top-down decision to execute a reduction in the workforce across the organization. We had experienced layoffs at Catalina before, and while they were never pleasant, I was always proud of how they were handled. Even going back to the early days when Catalina moved their headquarters from California to Florida and not all employees were able to keep their jobs, the leaders had exhibited care and concern for their people. Unfortunately, this time it was different. With the rush to execute the staff reduction and with all these new players leading teams they knew little about, the company was becoming unrecognizable to me. It was my first glimpse of an executive team that didn't appreciate or care as deeply for this company as I had hoped.

This was an extremely tough time, but I was determined to handle the actions and communications within my own organization with deep care for the company and compassion for the people. We had experienced other changes over the years, and I kept repeating these words to myself: "Change first the heart of the leader." I focused inwardly on how I was going to show up for my people and called a meeting with my leadership team to brief them on the situation before telling the remainder of my organization—over three hundred frightened individuals—that we had terminated almost 10 percent of our organization.

As I showed compassion for the team and specifically for the employees who were directly impacted, my goal was to lead the organization through this difficult time as best I could. It was a heartbreaking day. While my team appreciated my heart and care, they needed my strength and calmness first. It was up to me to be an example to the rest of the executive team of someone who minimized both the disruption to the business and the impact on the people involved.

It was more than clear that the digital transformation was going to be a large effort, one that this leadership team couldn't do without help. Catalina had very patient and supportive owners, and after considering the complexity of this work, they hired a consultant who sat this executive leadership team down to work on aligning the task at hand. During that first meeting, when the executive team sat in a conference room, the consultant put up a slide informing us that very few companies succeed at making a transformation such as the one we were attempting to accomplish. Talk about a wake-up call. We knew it was going to be difficult, but I wanted to know more about what we were facing so I could understand it.

SUCCESSFUL TRANSFORMATION

We went through an entire morning with the consultant, realizing the magnitude of what we were trying to do as it related to other companies making a similar shift. The two most critical principles for any successful transformation were (1) strong leadership and (2) a priority on engaging employees in the change all the way down to the front line. A sound strategy was important, but execution was the hardest part of a transformation, and it would only happen by following principles 1 and 2. It would require leaders to pay close attention to communicating clear goals, fostering collaboration, and building a strong vision for the future.

As we sat in the room, my peers would reference Netflix and how they handled their own shift to digital with an "out with the old, in with the new" model. Every one of those new executives sitting around the table had been sold on the idea of coming to Catalina with the goal of being part of the next Netflix story. They clearly wanted to be involved in a legendary success story and wanted to be able to say, "I helped accomplish that." Their motivation was a concern, and after listening further, I began to understand the nuts and bolts of the whole thing. Although the statistics said that 75 percent of companies survive a shift like this, the number is actually significantly smaller when you consider whether the transformation achieved or exceeded expectations. Only 5 percent of companies succeeded at a digital transformation with their expectations fulfilled.[1] It was up to the leaders in the organization, starting at the top, to beat those odds. It would require a significant change in not only the business model but in the leadership capabilities, mind-sets, and culture required to drive the change.

As I internalized this fact, I looked around the room and thought, "Oh my gosh, I don't know if we're going to be able to do this." All these new players were coming with their own ideas of what it would take to complete the transformation and their own expectations of the role they would play in the next greatest success story ever told.

How would these seemingly ego-driven leaders engage the company's people?

They were not focusing in on the culture or *how* we would lead through it. They were completely focused on changing the business model, the margins, how we delivered our product. All of that was important, but what about the deep culture that existed in the company? How would these seemingly ego-driven leaders engage the company's people? How would they touch their hearts?

That night, I went home and spent time thinking about everything I'd learned. Fairly new to my executive seat in the company I loved and still getting to know a new team, I was overwhelmed. Could this be done? After careful consideration, I realized that we could face this challenge. There was no way I could quit because the

---

1   These statistics have been pulled from Laurent-Pierre Baculard, Laurent Colombani, Virginie Flam, Ouriel Lancry, and Elizabeth Spaulding, "Orchestrating a Successful Digital Transformation," Bain & Company, November 22, 2017, https://www.bain.com/insights/orchestrating-a-successful-digital-transformation/.

organization was relying on me, and we had to prepare for what was to come. We had to be more intentional and aware about the people, the culture of the company, and the changing dynamics of the team. The company had a goal, but so did I. It became my role to be a reminder of what was so great about the culture of the company and to find ways to bring that history forward. We had worked so hard to cultivate the culture over the years, and in my mind it was essential to keep it in place as the transformation began. Those words that had stayed with me over the years, "Change first the heart of the leader," came to mind.

THE CULTURE CARRIER

Under the new leadership, it didn't take long before things began to fall apart. The CEO was removed from his role and an interim was brought in. The teams hadn't had a chance to absorb the reality and weight of the task at hand, and they weren't settled into any kind of groove yet. Everybody was operating in their own interests, thinking that they were aligned to the goal of digital transformation, but in reality, they weren't truly aligned because the how had not been addressed. We had all these individual leaders making their own decisions in their own functions and figuring out how they were going to get to the goal.

All of a sudden, long-tenured and knowledgeable employees were being pushed out and initiatives were shut down because they were too costly. It didn't matter that these initiatives were foundational to the transformation; it happened anyway. There was no one modeling the behavior that was needed or understanding that you must go deep to see what is going on to lead the people through this kind of change, make the right decisions, and get to the other side.

There were too many assumptions about how the business worked and too many broad-based decisions being made.

Our interim CEO was quick to assess what was going on: the need for slight modifications to the digital strategy and, more importantly, the fundamental shifts to be made in how this senior team was operating. He was brought in to take action and get things moving in the right direction while Catalina's board of directors searched for a permanent CEO. To my surprise and delight, this included a priority on team development and identifying and improving group behaviors that were hindering our ability to be an effective senior leadership team driving this transformation.

The CEO introduced us to *The Five Dysfunctions of a Team*, by Patrick Lencioni. The book is a fable about a female tech CEO facing the ultimate task of uniting a team in such disarray that it threatened to bring down the entire company. It felt eerily familiar, and I was struck by a profound quote from the book that represented the essence of what needed to be done: "If you could get all the people in an organization rowing in the same direction, you could dominate any industry, in any market, against any competition, at any time." I was sold and excited when the work began.

As an executive team, we started with trust, Lencioni's first step in the model, and soon moved on to conflict. Fortunately, there were signs of progress. Our CEO was modeling what he expected of his team and holding us accountable for the dysfunctional behaviors we needed to overcome. In addition to supporting this work as a team, he was connecting individually with each leader to assess risk and readiness across the organization against the transformation goals. Grateful for this type of leadership, and because my function was operating well, I spent my time with our interim CEO discussing the history and culture of Catalina and how this could be leveraged as an asset in the successful transformation. It was energizing to be given the opportunity to share more, and I felt validated that the emphasis and importance I had placed personally on the culture and the people as differentiators were recognized. I took this role of culture carrier seriously.

Drawing on what had worked for me in the past, influencing without direct reporting, I spent time trying to build relationships with each of the leaders, stepping outside my function to show them that there needed to be more education, more time for the people in the company to adjust and learn to make the changes required to succeed in the new digital world.

One of the first opportunities to see if this was working came quickly when we were faced with solving a major customer problem with the digital connectivity to their network. It required a cross-functional team to come together to solve the issue in the new digital environment of speed, agility, and transparency. It was an uncomfortably new place for many of our tenured employees, and it required the chief product officer, chief technology officer, and me to come together with one set of goals and expectations for this matrixed team.

We were still working through our own dysfunction, and it proved to be a chance to practice our executive team commitments of trust and productive conflict. We hashed out our differences before we entered the room, and when we got in front of the team, each of us had an equal role in communicating our expectations. The team solved the issue in record time, and we shared this as a case study for what could be accomplished when everyone from senior executive on down rows in the same direction.

DRIVING TRANSFORMATIONAL CHANGE

While progress was being made, these types of wins were few and far between. It was extremely frustrating because although I was building relationships and gaining respect, it was not enough. My peers saw the value in what I was trying to do, but when faced with the additional time and attention needed to engage with the ranks to support a different way of working, they dismissed me anyway, saying, "Okay, we get it. Now go do the job you were hired to do." I had no authority to force the behavior change, and the job of improving the team and leadership dynamics was very slow.

The pressures associated with gaining traction in digital and hitting the company's strategic milestones were frustrating for everyone, and the atmosphere became very chaotic. It was difficult just trying to keep my team insulated, keep the wheels on the bus, and minimize the impact that some of these misinformed, siloed decisions were having. The challenge was to drive transformational change in the short term while building skills and capabilities that would sustain the effectiveness and health of the organization long term. This would require leaders who would invest time engaging, developing, and leading—leading with heart. It was essential to keep things in balance between the organization and the people who were essential to its success. But it wasn't happening, and I had to figure out what I could do to keep the culture intact.

Just as I became even more committed to influencing the senior leadership and building on what little progress we had made in our effectiveness, using Lencioni's *The Five Dysfunctions*, a permanent CEO was hired. What little progress the team made under our interim CEO came to a halt as everyone was focused on building a new relationship with the new boss. The dynamics were once again unpredictable; everyone was acting in their own best interest and had their own agendas. Soon the collective behavior of this executive team, including the new CEO, was permeating down into the ranks, and organizational behaviors started changing. People who had been at Catalina for a very long time in different departments started acting differently than they had in the past. Long-tenured people in technology and finance who used to have really great relationships with those in operations and product began to fight and point fingers, emulating what they saw at the top. The organization was quickly headed toward adopting a dysfunctional, noncollaborative, out-for-yourself culture.

IN THE END

Fighting against the shift, I continued in my role as culture carrier within the company, trying to encourage collaboration and keep all the connections we had developed intact. Unfortunately, our new CEO handled communication very differently from his predecessors. These CEO changes were very disruptive not only to the leadership team but to the entire company. Three CEOs in three years during a time of significant change was simply too much for the organization to digest.

We were changing gears once again, and the chaos and disruption flowed from the top down. Although everyone was committed to the digital transformation, employees from the senior level down to the lowest level needed to be rallied. At this point, working harder than I'd ever worked in my life to keep things at my company in balance, I went for the company physical and everything changed.

CHAPTER 4

AN UNEXPECTED GLITCH

It was just a routine medical exam, and I had no expectations for receiving anything else but a clean bill of health. In fact, one of the reasons I signed on for the executive physical organized by my company was because I was concerned about my husband. We had only been married a year, and I was worried that adjusting to our new blended family as well as dealing with the stress of running his family business might be impacting his health. I thought it would be a good opportunity to have him checked out, so I dragged him along. As for me, I was only forty-four years old; was a health-conscious, active person; and felt just fine. I had no idea that within a few hours everything would change.

My husband and I arrived early that morning, and we were each quickly sent on our way to start the scheduled battery of tests and baselines. It wasn't long before I realized that something was wrong. First, an X-ray was taken and then a more detailed scan followed by a stress test for my heart and finally a heart ultrasound. As doctors and nurses came in and out of my room, my main concern was my daily schedule. There were other appointments scheduled for that day, and I was starting to miss them. Finally, I said, "Hey, I've got a schedule to keep. What's going on?"

That's when they told me, "Something doesn't look right, and we have to talk."

Immediately, I sensed the seriousness of the situation and asked them to find my husband, who was in another part of the hospital. The doctors sat us both down, and we canceled all other appointments for the day. During the testing they found two congenital health issues—as if one wasn't enough! There was a tumor in my chest that they believed to be malignant and a hole in my heart not detected since birth. They discovered that my heart was extremely enlarged on the right side, and my body had been compensating for it my entire life, which is an amazing thing when you think about it.

MY DIAGNOSIS

After the initial shock of hearing my diagnosis, there was a calmness that came over me, and immediately, as if I was on autopilot, I went into crisis planning. Though I didn't realize it then, the influence of my mom's response to my dad's diagnosis so many years ago was apparent. It was like I went into crisis-management mode to figure out what I needed to do next. How would I communicate with my family when I had such limited information? I'd be going back for more tests, but what would I tell them in the meantime?

Despite my loyalty to my job, my family and my health had to be

Despite my loyalty to my job, my family and my health had to be put at the forefront.

put at the forefront. Leaving the hospital that day, I began internalizing what was happening and tried to come up with a plan of action. At that point, I thought the tumor was most likely cancerous and knew that I had to come up with a crisis plan to get us through what I thought was coming next.

Over the next two weeks, I went back for tests seven times, which led to my having open-heart surgery to remove the tumor and repair the hole. Within thirty days of finding out that I had a tumor in my chest and a hole in my heart, I found myself lying on an operating table facing open-heart surgery. The operation was a success; I was one of the lucky ones. But life as I knew it was over, and it was time to look toward an unfamiliar but welcome future.

During the crisis, I was determined to understand what this whole situation was trying to tell me. Mindful of my thoughts, I was willing to explore what lessons I should be learning from this experience. Always curious and open to new thinking, I came out on the other side of this life-threatening situation but knew it was a pivotal point in my life. It was very clear to me that I was being told that I needed to make changes in my life, to reevaluate the role I was in, and rethink my seventy-hour work week as a way of life.

As I awoke in the intensive care unit, the first thing I said was "Where's the camera?" I'd made it to the other side, and my family was with me. Throughout this journey I had been very mindful of what this experience was trying to tell me, but I also wanted to understand what my family was experiencing from where they sat. Before I went into the surgery, I had begun journaling and made my husband promise that he would take pictures throughout my recovery and document everything. It was important for me to learn from this second chance, really experience the journey as well as the recovery process.

Shortly after that first day in the ICU, we received news that the tumor was calcified and that I didn't have cancer. Coming out unscathed was a big relief since going into it, we thought the diagnosis would not be a good one. It was a best-case scenario, but I wanted to know what the message was. What was this health scare trying to tell me? Was it a sign that I should not go back to the way things were? Did I need to make some major changes? This realization was the beginning of the next phase of my life, my second chance.

MY PLAN OF ACTION

A planful person cannot help but immediately begin to map out the next move, and that's exactly what I did. First, I had to get out of the hospital, focus forward even more, and figure out what the next chapter was for me. At the forefront of my mind was that this was a second chance, but it was also about putting my family front and center. This was a catalyst, but there were other things going on. My son would soon be entering high school, and there would only be a short window of time to spend with him before he'd be driving himself around and never be home. We had two more years of carpool where he'd be stuck in the car with me and I could connect with him without interruption.

And there was my husband to think about. He was working on opening a new store, and his business was really taking off. There were a lot of things influencing what my path would be, and I needed to consider all of them: family, career, health, and discovering exactly what this experience was trying to tell me.

During my eight-week recovery period, I was not working, but the outreach from my work family was tremendous. Although I was out of the building for a period of time, focusing on my health and recovery, the business continued to run since I had mentored and coached the team to a place where they were able to carry on without me. That was my first real taste of seeing the impact that my passion for team and leadership development had on such a large scale. My people were prepared to drive the business forward while maintaining the company culture and were able to continue despite my absence. My recovery went well, and when it was time to return to work, it was the thought of connecting with my teams and expressing how proud I was of them that excited me, not the work I was missing.

A NEW PERSPECTIVE

Once I was released to go back to work and returned to the leadership role I had left eight weeks prior, I noticed right away that I had a different perspective on things. The amount of energy and effort spent to collaborate with my peers, influence decisions, and essentially pick up where I had left off in the role I had played before were unbalanced compared to the progress being made against the transformation. I knew in my heart it wasn't worth the trade-off for the time I was spending away from my family. What if I could channel that energy and effort toward my passion of leadership development, coaching, and mentoring? I could make a bigger impact. This is when I made the decision to wind down my career and exit the company. It was quite difficult because of the people I'd come to know and the wonderful relationships we had. It meant everything to me to preserve the culture we'd created, and since the teams had functioned well in my absence, I believed that even without my presence, the impact would still be there. I was now faced with the difficult task of cutting ties with a company I loved and had worked with for more than two decades. Could I do it?

No one questioned why I'd come to the conclusion that I had to leave; everyone knew what I'd been through, so it wasn't much of a shock. The company was still in the midst of this tough transformation, and that was weighing on a lot of people. There was chaos and change fatigue going on in the organization, so from that perspective it wasn't that tough to follow through on my decision to exit. Once I informed the senior team that I'd be leaving, I expected that we would begin the conversation about planning how they would deal with my resignation.

Instead they said, "Oh, you don't really mean that. You've just had a rough time. What if we gave you more time? What if we let you ease back in? What if we changed your role? Do you want to do something else? We don't want you to leave. Think about this, think about that, think about this."

That was really hard because I was secure in my decision going in, but once faced with the reality of actually leaving after twenty-five years, it became very difficult. My head started swirling, and I began to second-guess my thinking and my reasons for leaving. Fear was creeping in. It was important to keep coming back to why I'd made the decision in the first place and to trust the signs that were there. This was an intentional decision, and I had to keep telling myself to face my fear and move on.

I held my ground. The company accepted that I'd be leaving and said they supported me despite being unable to convince me to stay. They brought up the optics of the organization because they knew my leaving was going to send a ripple through a company that was in transition, a company that was suffering change fatigue. The executive team knew I represented hope in where the company was going and that I had a calming effect on the entire organization. How would they close the gap?

Of course, I was worried for the future of the company and certainly didn't want to be perceived as someone who was abandoning ship. Although most people understood why I was leaving, there were some that didn't seem to get it. My only hope was that the care and concern for the culture and behaviors so critical to leading people through such a big change would continue to be a focus after I was gone.

PREPARING FOR DEPARTURE

As I prepared for my departure, I remained committed to the transformation and continued to share my hope for a bright future, staying aware of and sensitive to the optics. I agreed on a long exit; I told them in May that I'd be leaving but offered to stay through December. It was difficult on a personal level, but it was the right thing to do—or so I felt at the time. When I'd made my decision to leave, the new CEO was settled in and had announced a couple of shifts in the company strategy. Like many times before, there was initial excitement around the new ideas, the shiny pennies as I called them.

It was May, the same month that I shared with the CEO that I would be leaving, when they brought the top fifty leaders from all countries together for a meeting to create alignment and buy-in to these new initiatives. It was my global operations team that was asked to drive a new initiative: the development of a customer-experience strategy. It was a reflection of their amazing talents and the strong leadership skills they'd developed over the years. It was also a great distraction from the fact that I would be leaving as I passed the torch to this qualified and passionate group of people. What a vote of confidence and recognition of their contributions.

STAYING MOTIVATED

Unfortunately, during my six-month wind down, there was little progress in the digital transformation, and the implementation of our new initiatives was complicated and slow. Since the company did not broadly announce my planned departure until October, there were those who doubted my intentions, figuring that I must have known something and was aware of the serious trouble the business was in. Of course, I knew the company was struggling, but I never knew they were on the verge of bankruptcy when I informed them of my resignation. During this time, I continued to remain very focused on finding a way to keep teams motivated and preserve the culture of care after I was gone.

My focus was mainly on the people and getting strong succession in place; however, I still worried about making sure that the people felt like they could carry on the culture without me. After the organization announced that I was leaving, there were many personal, one-on-one conversations. Once I had talked to as many people as I could, they really understood my decision for leaving and knew it was not a reflection of the company or the leadership in place. It really was a personal decision to reprioritize things in my life and make a difference in an even bigger way.

When people started using the word *legacy* to describe the impact of my leadership, it was truly amazing. The word *legacy* really stuck with me because it was a consistent theme, and believe me, it was quite humbling. I'd always taken the responsibility that came with being a leader seriously, but I had no idea that people viewed me this way. People were talking about my journey, starting in an entry-level position and moving up the ranks as I tried different things.

"No one does that anymore," they said. "Who does that?"

It was a little uncomfortable for me, and I never wanted the attention to be focused in my direction. My goals were to get through the wind down and then quietly exit stage left. I planned to do a little consulting with the company over the next few months and then continue to move forward. That was my preference. I didn't want a party or any fanfare. I waited until the last weekend before cleaning out my office to quietly depart, but the feedback that people were sharing was overwhelming, and my departure was going to be more impactful than I had originally thought. The business would continue, and the operations wouldn't skip a beat, but there was a lot of talk about the how. How was it going to be run without my presence and leadership? Would there be other leaders who appreciated the deep history and cared enough to step in and carry it through?

LEAVING A LEGACY OF HEART

The word *legacy* kept creeping back into my mind and confirmed that this style of leadership, using heart, compassion, and authenticity, would leave a mark. I was leaving a legacy and only after I reflected did I understand that this was unique.

But why be a legacy leader? If you accept the challenge and acknowledge that your role as a leader is a privilege, there are three very specific reasons it is worth the effort to lead with heart and leave a legacy.

First, you've met the minimum price of entry in getting to where you are by demonstrating skills, capabilities, and competence in getting the job done. You have high accountability and a strong desire to achieve success. As a legacy leader, you can have an exponential impact on the success of the business and the people through your ability to drive results and outcomes through other people. You already know what it's like to be successful, and being a legacy leader allows you to multiply that through others.

The second reason is that you get to live out your personal leadership brand. Not many leaders get to experience authentic leadership. When you're a legacy leader, you are rewarded with the knowledge that you've done self-reflection and found the sweet spot where you operate at your best. You are performing at your personal best, and when you operate that way, build the skills, and evolve that personal leadership brand, you can take it wherever you go. It transcends whatever you're going to do next if it's done right.

> *When you're a legacy leader, you are rewarded with the knowledge that you've done self-reflection and found the sweet spot where you operate at your best.*

The final reason for striving to become a legacy leader is that you will play an important role in helping others do their best work. You get to help others find their *why*, and you connect with them for a purpose beyond your own success. You leave your mark and leave things better than how you found them.

A legacy leader is an inspiration for others and can look back on how they've impacted an organization. Businesses come and go, and people will rewrite the history of a company's results and how the organization got to where it was, good or bad. Others may take the credit or might remember things differently, but what people can't change is how they felt about you as a leader and the hand you had in their own experiences, their personal growth and success.

As my last day approached, my team assured me that they would continue what we had created and that they would make me proud. We gathered together to renew our team values and collaborated with all the members of our organization to collectively come up with the phrase "Think, act, be kind." They committed to carrying forward and leading with heart.

I received a number of wonderful messages after I left, and one in particular stood out. It was from one of my amazing colleagues; she made the commitment to do her best to continue to stay true to her authentic self. She told me that she would continue to lead with heart and keep the team engaged through the uncertainty and challenges they were facing. It felt wonderful to know that I was able to influence her, and I continued to give her encouragement and support even after leaving. This experience shortly after I left reinforced for me that although I no longer worked for Catalina, I could continue to help people in this new stage of my life.

NEW GOAL

My new goal was to follow my passion for leadership development and pursue leadership coaching. Coaching was a way to draw on my own leadership experiences and help develop possibilities in others that they might not see in themselves. I left my company, set new goals, and shifted my mind-set toward the future. Soon, I started hearing from my network of people; they asked me if I was interested in working for them and would often tell me that they had something I would be interested in. Although I would not be stepping back into the corporate world, there might be a way I could help them. My new life as a coach was my new beginning.

CHAPTER 5

LOTS OF LESSONS
AND *NO* REGRETS

After my departure from Catalina, a lot of people started contacting me and asking me to share my secrets. Reflecting on the past twenty-five years, I knew what I had discovered could benefit others, so eventually I came up with seven leadership lessons and shared them on a blog. It was amazing to see how so many years at the same company could culminate in just a few key points about leadership. My experiences, pain, failures, and successes became the basis for my personal leadership brand and the reason why I was recognized as a legacy leader. Here's what it boils down to:

1. **Authenticity is underrated.** Early in my career, I was told that in order to be successful I should just "act like a man." Really? Regardless of what is required by an organization, the best leaders find a way to stay true to their values, beliefs, *and* style. Whatever it is for you, honor yourself by

engaging in the world around you, internalizing what is going on, and listening to your heart.

2. **Servant leadership isn't just another buzz phrase.** Selfless leaders lead for the organization and bleed for others in the company, not for their own egos. Doing this will return ten times what you put in—I promise.

3. **Laughter is the best medicine.** How you show up every day sets the tone. You don't always realize the impact a smile or a laugh will have on others.

4. **Bring others along.** You can have a culture of collaboration without consensus building, and you might be surprised how a little effort—checking in, asking questions, and encouraging discussion—goes a long way with empowering teams and building trust.

5. **Be their champion.** That is your job. The higher up in the organization you go, the less work you really do. Your job is to be looking out for your team and creating the forums and the environment for them to do their best work.

6. **Be kind.** People remember how you made them feel. Will there be days you are angry, disappointed, or overwhelmed? Yes. Be kind anyway. The smallest act of kindness or appreciation makes a long, lasting impression.

7. **Find your voice.** Others want to hear what you have to say. Have confidence to walk into that room and contribute. For some, it is about filling air space, but the best leaders show up ready with their unique, authentic perspective.

These lessons are anchored by one important practice: ***be intentional in the* how**. *How* you show up each day, *how* you engage with others, *how* you lead. As mentioned before, this was the style of leadership that people responded to and that helped me leave a legacy.

Yes, there have been many books written about leadership. People speak of great leaders and not-so-great leaders and the impact that they have on an organization's ability to succeed. I have found that it is just as important to be able to recognize the characteristics and behaviors of a bad leader as well as a great one. Ineffective leaders lack self-awareness; they can't self-regulate, and as a result, they let their own fears and insecurities take over. Their behavior tends to be ego-based. They take credit for their team's work, they focus too much on their own success, and they often create an environment of fear and intimidation.

Can this be fixed? Are there ways for someone to change how they present themselves, to start acting for others, modeling for others, championing them, and connecting to them? And if an ego-driven leader is presented with solutions for change, are they willing to *actually do it?*

THE CENTER OF SUCCESS

To be successful for the long haul for a team or company, you must put others at the center of that success. Your role as a leader is to realize that the work is about the people and what they need. Think of it like a puzzle, where the strengths of individuals are the pieces put into place to create a whole. People should be put where they can do their best work, and if that place doesn't exist, you should work to create it. One colleague spoke of the importance of being stretched under my leadership, of being put in situations that made her uncomfortable but knowing that I'd had faith she would ride through the challenge. I believed in her even if she didn't believe in herself. There is no place for ego in this style of leadership.

Some leaders leave a legacy for the wrong reasons; they make their mark but in a way that doesn't drive business outcomes, doesn't leave others inspired, and doesn't lift them up to help them do their best work. An ego-driven leader who desires to take all the credit and be a solo act often displays the following characteristics:

- lacks either the desire or the skills to collaborate with others;

- discounts other points of view and misses opportunities to bring people along in the change or in the thought process;

- leads with fear, jumps to conclusions, and passes judgment;

- allows emotion and their own insecurities to drive decisions and behaviors;

- doesn't listen to their employees and isn't open to feedback; and

- overlooks the occasion to go deep into the business, to truly understand and appreciate the concept of "go slow to go fast."

I am sure we have all seen these leadership behaviors in our past. It's important to recognize them, as they slow progress and can even derail an organization working toward the goal.

At my company, many of the leaders were hired with a specific mission in mind: as an additive or an extension of the collective skills that are needed for organizational success. Although they may have been very well-intentioned people, they were coming from their own paradigm and expertise. In most cases, they weren't equipped to really show up, to engage with others, and to lead one team with one voice.

This is so critical to a company's success, especially a company that's going through such a dramatic transformation. Ineffective leaders can mean well but often aren't equipped to show up, to engage with others, and to lead with heart. In my experience, I have seen how the collective abilities, beliefs, and behaviors of a company's leadership team will drive either success or failure. The most effective leadership hinges on a desire to develop possibilities for others and help them do their best work.

> *The most effective leadership hinges on a desire to develop possibilities for others and help them do their best work.*

INSPIRATIONAL LEADERSHIP

In examining what I have seen in my own experiences, I have developed several approaches in my own coaching practice. Driven by the fact that I had a broad and deep impact on my company for twenty-five years, I was inspired by the thought of helping other organizations and individual leaders become their best possible selves. Thinking back to my beginnings at Catalina, I was inspired by the entrepreneurial spirit and passion they had as a start-up company. Seeing their ideas come to life and working in that kind of environment sparked such a passion in me that my job never felt like work. Surely everyone else around me felt the same way, right? Turns out they didn't. How could I help them get that same feeling of being engaged and excited to do their best work?

Inspirational leadership became very important to me while I was moving up the ranks because it was something I had experienced firsthand, and I wanted other people to experience it also. It is a gift to be inspired, and there are times in your career where you have to look a little harder for inspiration or even create your own at times. It is a leader's job to be inspired and be inspiring every day. Inspiration looks different for everyone, so it's important to have an open mind. My focus was on how my employees would be able to connect and engage in their work, keeping in mind that everyone is different. What inspired me is not necessarily what will inspire you, but inspiration for you to do your best work is very important.

Most of my time was spent developing my leaders and creating an environment that was inspirational, one that helped people see where they were going, gave them hope for the future, and showed them how they could connect but did not dictate to them how they were going to do that. It boiled down to creating a feeling and engaging the heart in an authentic way. Being in an inspired environment creates the opportunity for people to individually, and as a team, push harder to achieve the high standards they have for themselves and the business. This is what gets results.

There was a time when I was asked to present at an all-employee meeting in front of 1,200 people. As part of a cross-functional team that was asked to look at competitive threats to the business, we were tasked with making recommen-

> *Being in an inspired environment creates the opportunity for people to individually, and as a team, push harder to achieve the high standards they have for themselves and the business. This is what gets results.*

dations for a new company mission. Someone on the team had to present our work to the organization, and I drew the short straw—no problem. It was an opportunity to inspire rather than to just stand up at a meeting and say, "Okay, here's what we did. Here's our analysis." Instead, I presented it in a way that connected personally and individually, describing how each employee would feel walking into the building each day when aligned to this new mission.

THE GREAT CONNECTION

After the presentation, I received an enormous number of emails and texts, with the majority of them coming from females in the organization. While the connection that I created with employees in different departments and at different levels was impactful, I was struck by the reaction of the women. That was when I realized that it was okay to personalize the message in a way that brought emotion and feeling to the business. It wasn't viewed as weak; on the contrary, they appreciated seeing a woman's strength and presence and were engaged by and connected to the message because of its passion and authenticity. Wanting to be an inspiration for everyone, I modeled and showed other females that it was possible to make an impact by being yourself and reflecting what you feel in your heart.

The reality is that there are a lot of women functioning within male-dominated environments, and if a female speaks her mind and is assertive, she can get a reputation for being "too much" and scaring people off. On the other hand, if she is quiet and reflective, she takes the chance of never being perceived as someone who could be a leader. It was important for me to do my best and be a role model for other females, showing them that there are different ways of being effective while remaining authentic and following your heart.

There will always be things that everybody needs to work on, whether it's communication or presentation skills, assertiveness or strategic thinking. There are always opportunities for leadership development, but the beauty of having a team is diversity. There's diversity in team members' talents, experiences, and approaches. I haven't worked with one team yet that wouldn't benefit from learning to create the right forum for that diversity to do its best work. Based on the feedback received from the females in my company, I made it my goal to continue to inspire them to be their authentic, best selves. Approaching your leadership role in this way makes the job of leading with heart that much easier.

CHAPTER 6

THE HEART OF THE MATTER

When I think back over my leadership career, I am proud of the involvement my leaders had with their employees and families. A particular example comes to mind of an accomplished leader and critical member of our organization who was hit with a crisis during her pregnancy. She ended up in the hospital, and we all scrambled to keep everything on track. After the crisis passed, she was put on bed rest for the remainder of her pregnancy. She was known for being highly accountable and always focused on getting things done right, so it was no surprise she wanted to keep working. Our first reaction was "Absolutely not!" We wanted her to take time to stay healthy and be with her family. The most important thing was to have a healthy baby.

However, she was concerned about her family medical leave starting at the time the bed rest started and was afraid of losing her time with the baby after it was born. She asked for our help. We came up with a plan that allowed her to do some work from her hospital bed—light-duty kind of stuff—so that she could have the time she needed with her baby once it was born. She was a valued member of our work family, and we treated her with the same heart we would treat any member of our own families.

Today's workforce expects to establish personal, one-to-one relationships that show someone cares and appreciates the work they are doing. Leaders are a vital factor in creating this connection, and when I think back to the early days at Catalina, I see that the founders were great at this. A strong personal connection between the founders and the employees showed itself in a myriad of ways.

MAKING PERSONAL CONNECTIONS

Every year at our Christmas party, one of the founders would put up a chart comparing the number of babies that were born to our employees with the growth line of the company. He would say, "I want more babies this year! I love it when our employees have babies. It's the greatest thing ever because sales go up!" It was always funny, but at the same time, it set the tone early on for just how engaged our founders were with their people. We were at a holiday party. We were reflecting on the prior year and how great we did, and at the same time we were making a personal connection to how the individuals and the families contributed to that. It was one of the things that was just so important, and it stuck with me.

As we continued to grow and as my organization got larger, there were a lot of people on my teams that were in their childbearing years, and there were many babies being born. We loved it even though it seemed we were always juggling baby showers and maternity leaves. It was great when we had smooth deliveries and healthy babies being born. The first time we had a situation where a member of a team had a crisis with a pregnancy, we worked very hard to show care and compassion. Here they were dealing with a real scare, and they needed reassurance that we had their backs.

The way we handled our employees and events in their personal lives that impacted their ability to work came from the roots the company had set down when it was first established. The tone was arrived at early on, and I had the

Here they were dealing with a real scare, and they needed reassurance that we had their backs.

privilege to be able to have seen that in action over the years. Even as the company grew, my commitment to following the spirit the founders had set at the very start, keeping in mind that the people were at the heart of the company, never ended. At the end of the day, the most important thing of all is your people.

DON'T LOSE HEART, OR ELSE

One of the biggest trends influencing the growth strategies for many service organizations is the customer experience. The belief is that the customer is the heart of your business and their desires and preferences come before all else. Customer satisfaction is a differentiator for companies because it's the customers who buy your products. However, the pressing question for many leaders facing this challenge is, Who comes first, customer or employee? There is a good argument to be made that if you take care of your employees first, then they'll take better care of your customers and your business will grow.

Richard Branson, founder of the Virgin Group, insists that clients do not come first but that employees do. He believes that if you take care of your employees, they will take care of your clients.

This belief was embedded in the culture of Catalina from the early days. Family and employees came first. If they were taken care of with heart, the business and the customers would also be taken care of. People are the heart of the matter, and they're critical for the success of an organization. They're a multiplier for the organization's success. Put people first, and everything else will follow. Don't lose heart or else the company will head for trouble.

After I left Catalina, things started to change. As mentioned earlier in the book, there were so many different leadership styles and a succession of CEOs that caused things to really pivot. Those changes got the company off track, and they stopped putting their people first, which eventually led to their demise. The whole environment changed, and employees became more fearful. They were told they were part of the old regime, were old school, or didn't have the capability to make the digital transformation. Fear and dissension began to form between teams because of the heavy lifting involved in the transformation process.

The leaders that had been brought in weren't aligned with how the company was going to operate, and as a result, there was less collaboration. People were embracing the "It's not my job" mentality, so the lines started to become drawn, and the work environment rapidly began to change. When people's livelihoods are threatened, they become defensive and protective as team spirit is replaced by self-preservation. The teams that were set up to function a certain way began

When people's livelihoods are threatened, they become defensive and protective as team spirit is replaced by self-preservation.

to fall apart, and people put their energy into protecting themselves and their jobs.

The competition in this new digital age was fierce, and as a result, the need to get the transformation completed was urgent. Start-up companies were popping up left and right with digital solutions for everything. What made this specific transformation so difficult was that we had a thirty-five-year-old business that was built on a traditional foundation for marketing. It was a proprietary network that made switching to digital akin to trying to turn the *Titanic* on a dime.

For years, the company had navigated the marketing waters that no one else could touch. There wasn't a lot of competition, but then suddenly you need to change course so you don't hit the iceberg and sink. The whole situation was compounded by the intricacies associated with the technology, with the relationships Catalina had built, and how they were integrated with their retailers' systems. They had well-established expectations with their clients regarding how they did business. It wasn't like starting from scratch and building something up. They were forced to redesign and reestablish themselves, and that added to the difficulty.

Despite the fact that when I left my team was very committed to carrying on the leadership culture we had created, these obstacles proved too much even for such dedicated people. When they realized that it wasn't about the people anymore, decisions started being made out of desperation. Team members who had hoped to be their own culture carriers were forced to begin making their own personal decisions. The company leadership had lost heart, and the results were catastrophic.

WHAT IS HEART?

Leaders with heart have presence, are present, and show concern for individuals on their teams. They listen to employees' needs, show compassion, create shared dreams for the future, and create opportunities for them to experience success. Having heart is about knowing what employees need to feel fulfilled by cultivating personal human connections. That's what heart looks like. Leaders with heart do two things really well:

Show up with intention. Leaders with heart adopt a "people first, company second" mind-set. They project a sense of responsibility and commitment to their employees, own the culture, and model the behavior they want people to follow. They have congruence with the organization's values and their own. They strive to build credibility and gain the respect of others.

Engage with intention. Every interaction can have an impact. Leaders with heart demonstrate an interest in their employees and get to know them personally. They get to the core of what inspires, motivates, and connects people individually—and identify what touches their hearts.

ESSENTIAL WAYS TO LEAD WITH HEART

We have defined leading with heart and understand that the *how* is very important: how you show up and how you engage with others. I have developed a leadership development model that further defines what this looks like.

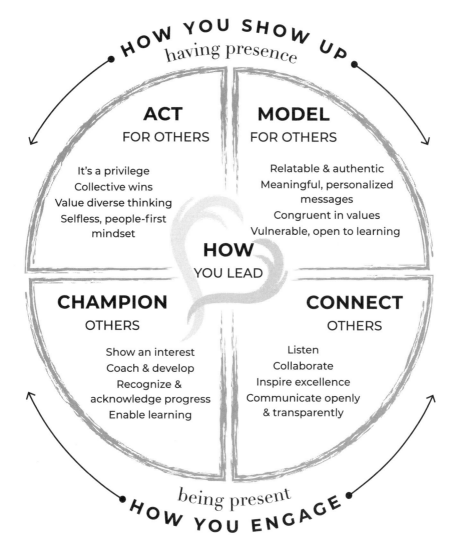

While this provides a framework, there are millions of ways to be recognized as a leader with heart, one who leaves a legacy. It is so important that your approach is authentic and comfortable for you. When you intentionally lead from a place of authenticity, then in times of chaos and adversity, regardless of the situation, having all the answers or not, dealing with the complex and messy, you come from a place of confidence, maturity, and strength. You have the resolve to lead with purpose, courage, and heart.

Many leaders are at a pivotal point, and while they have done a good job so far, they are faced with the business environment of today that is requiring them to raise the bar—to lead in a different way, to create value to their organizations and teams in a new way. How can you recognize and embrace what makes you unique as a leader and use your personal leadership style to engage the hearts and minds of your people? Remember, the best gifts you can give the world are the ones that come most naturally to you.

I have created a visual of the leadership behaviors that I have seen and experienced over the years and the gap that exists between those leaders who just get by and those leaders who intentionally engage the hearts and minds of their people, those leaders who lead with heart. This framework provides a better picture of what it looks like at the point of arrival. Each of us is on our own personal leadership journey, and you may be further along on your path to do your best work. Think about where you are on this path and how, as a leader, you are moving *from* → *to*.

HOW YOU SHOW UP

FROM	→	TO
"It's a right."	→	"It's a privilege."
Solo act	→	Collective wins
Closed minded	→	Open minded
Controlling of how you are perceived	→	Relatable and authentic
Transactional, scripted in information sharing	→	Meaningful, personalized messages from the heart and from experience
Ego driven, self first	→	Selfless, people first

Inconsistent in beliefs and actions	→	Congruent in values, "walk the talk"
All knowing and fearful of failure	→	Vulnerable, treats mistakes as lessons, open to learning

HOW YOU ENGAGE OTHERS

FROM	→	TO
Does most of the talking	→	Does most of the listening
Directive	→	Collaborative
Demands results, controls outcomes	→	Inspires excellence, creates forums for their best work
Doesn't engage, keeps it to business	→	Shows an interest, makes personal connections
Steps in, does it for them	→	Stretches them, coaches and develops
Hidden agendas and shrouded in mystery	→	Shares thought process, communicates openly and transparently
Overlooks accomplishments	→	Acknowledges progress and recognizes small wins
Punitive, culture of fear	→	Encourages failure and learning, culture of trust

Being aware and leveraging your own personal leadership style gives you the courage to engage with others authentically, build trust with your team, and enable them to leverage their own strengths to make a more powerful whole. This is fundamental to being a leader with heart who will bring immeasurable benefits to yourself and your organization.

CHAPTER 7

VOICE OF THE PEOPLE

Imagine a room filled with over four hundred people attending a company meeting. Most are there in person, with a handful attending remotely. Now imagine that many of these people are feeling weighed down by the fatigue caused by all the changes going on in the company. This was the scenario I found myself facing as one of their leaders, and I had to do something to turn this around and make it better. These meetings typically took place about four times a year and were used to update employees about the business and to do some general recognition work.

However, with things being the way they were, it was essential to do something to reassure them, inspire them, and give them the confidence to keep going. There was an opportunity to use this particular meeting to be vulnerable, to share my own thoughts and feelings as their leader, as someone who was also feeling the heavy effects of all the change.

Sensing they had lost their connection to why we were on this journey and feeling that they were just heads down doing the work, I acknowledged that I found myself going from meeting to meeting, always looking down at my phone and not taking the time to be aware of the people walking in the hall, riding the elevator, or catching up outside the breakroom. I myself had my head down just trying to get through each chaotic day. It was up to me to take an opportunity to recognize this about myself and share my feelings with them.

My own behavior wasn't sitting well with me and didn't model the leadership or create the environment that I knew was especially important during this tumultuous time. I couldn't promise them that we were done with the change, that things would get easier, that they could slow their pace and "go back to normal," but I could pledge to them that even as I was running from meeting to meeting with my hair on fire, I would put my phone in my pocket and take every opportunity to connect with people even for the briefest moment.

TAKE ADVANTAGE OF THE MOMENTS

Yes, we were really busy and had so much to get done. All of us were overcommitted in our own way, but this was an opportunity for me to be more aware of my surroundings, lift my head up, and take a moment, even if it was while running through the hallway, to interact with people. A quick smile, a moment of connection—even the briefest connection—was important. Putting the phone away and taking these small moments to connect showed people that they were important to me and that they mattered. I felt better doing this, and it was a way to acknowledge people and model an approachable and consistent presence that was so essential during this critical time where everyone was just really tired and looking to get through the day.

By this point in my career, I had hosted hundreds of management meetings and town halls and knew that some had hit the mark, while some didn't. However, this particular time was an opportunity to get in front of this organization and inspire them. It was time to send the message that while we usually followed an agenda in these meetings, I understood that wasn't what they needed at this time. I needed to engage their hearts by acknowledging what I knew they were feeling and being vulnerable enough to share that I was feeling it too. My promise to find other ways to connect with them, even if it was nonverbal, such as simply making eye contact or smiling as we passed in the hallway, was sending a message that I was there in the present moment and in it with them.

HIT THE RESET BUTTON

When my own behavior change started to happen, it resonated with many people and with my senior leadership team in particular. They shared their own feelings with me, and we talked about how we had all been behaving. It was a great chance for me to model a different behavior, and my leadership team followed suit. By hitting the reset button, it allowed me and my team to find additional opportunities that would engage our teams in conversation and let us hear feedback. We were seeking out the voices of the people who worked for us, and because of the shift in my own behavior, I began hearing those voices.

The Thanksgiving holiday weekend was over when I walked onto the elevator and simply smiled and said hello to everyone. It turned out that one of the women I said hello to worked in our call center.

Now keep in mind that it was Thanksgiving time, and we had team members on call 24/7. We had systems in place that ensured there was coverage for our top customers, and our leaders were watching metrics over the weekend to make sure things were continuing to operate as expected.

We were feeling really good after reviewing all our metrics from the weekend and were thrilled that Black Friday weekend was a success. Then I spoke to Mary from the call center. The simple act of smiling at her and saying hello gave her the confidence to speak to me about her experience over the long holiday weekend.

She said to me, "Although the weekend was a success by the metrics, there was a bug in the system." She had logged into the system at 12:00 a.m., 3:00 a.m., and 5:00 a.m. to make sure things were working behind the scenes. She stayed on it, checking the queue. It turned out there was a delay with our offshore team, and they couldn't fix it, so Mary went above and beyond to close the gap with another team over the weekend. It was her staying up basically all night, checking the queue, and keeping things moving that kept things working so nothing was noticeable to the customer. All of this would have gone unnoticed if we'd relied only on the metrics. Things weren't operating as smoothly as they appeared to be, and as it turned out, it was because of this highly engaged and dedicated person on our team that the holiday weekend was a success.

ACKNOWLEDGE CONTRIBUTIONS

Future successes were linked back to this employee because, by sharing her experiences, she gave us an opportunity to make improvements in our process and our communication across teams. More importantly, it was an opportunity to make sure that this frontline employee was heard and her contributions noticed. This is just one example of something that came out of being aware, approachable, and present.

Being more present and intentional in how I showed up as a leader was just what the team needed. When things are hectic and chaotic and people are super busy, it's easy for any leader to get to the point where they are breathing what I call "rarefied air." It becomes hard for a leader, especially a leader in charge of a large organization, to maintain connections to the truth of what's really going on. It becomes easy to gloss over some things, but I was determined to be a leader who was more present and aware in order to combat this idea of breathing in my own fumes, this rarefied air.

Something as simple as a brief moment helped me take the time to put myself in others' shoes, to understand what they were feeling and experiencing. By helping them make sense of their circumstances, leaders allow them to engage in a way that channels their feedback, ideas, and even complaints into something productive. Although it wasn't great to hear that we had problems that Thanksgiving weekend, we could channel that in a productive way and help increase the engagement in the organization and ultimately achieve a better business outcome.

Develop Possibility

Don't ever underestimate the impact that employees who feel connected to the business and the leadership can have. They will start to see new possibilities for themselves to contribute and make a measurable difference, while you as a legacy leader will leave your mark in the service of others by helping them feel and be successful. There are specific things you can do to help your people draw out the possibility and potential they don't always see for themselves: empower them, develop them, and learn from them.

EMPOWER YOUR PEOPLE

The most empowered teams work for leaders who motivate, coach, and engage them so they become more self-reliant and independent in their decisions. Those leaders who create an opportunity for ownership and encourage a sense of pride in the work create a fundamental shift in how teams and leaders operate, which is ultimately a catalyst in developing a culture of empowerment. The best illustration of this happens in service organizations that are in the business of meeting and exceeding customer expectations.

Southwest Airlines is a great example of a company that has empowered employees to use their talents and skills to solve problems in real time rather than asking for permission to do something that would satisfy and maintain loyalty among their customers. It was interesting to find out how they've held this culture for so many years. How did it start? How has it been maintained? It began with their founder, Herb Kelleher, who made a point to personally connect with as many people as possible, and he did it one on one when the company was small. As the company grew, Kelleher couldn't connect one on one anymore, but he had established an expectation that the leaders were going to engage with the employees and make building human connections a priority. They found the right forums and ways to share this philosophy among all the leaders, so as the network grew, they still had a finger on the pulse of how people were feeling.

Southwest has empowered their employees in a multitude of ways. All you have to do is look at their tagline to know their philosophy: "Without a heart, it's just a machine." (The machine refers to their planes.) Even their logo is a heart, so they literally have a heart on the belly of each and every one of their aircraft. If you do a quick search online, you'll find hundreds of examples of how Southwest's empowered employees have made a difference, but one particular story stands out for me.

In 2011 an Arizona man was traveling on business when he received a call that his two-year-old grandson was going to be taken off life support that evening. He needed to fly to Denver immediately to have a chance to see his grandson before he died. The man's wife booked him on the next available flight. Unfortunately, the grandfather was delayed getting through security in Los Angeles, and it became clear he wasn't going to make his flight. His wife called Southwest and explained the gravity of the situation, asking them if there was anything they could do. When the man finally got through security and arrived at his gate, he was twelve minutes late. Thinking that he had missed the flight, he was stunned when he saw the door to the Jetway open and the pilot standing beside it waiting for him. Southwest is tremendous at empowering their employees to make decisions on behalf or for the betterment of the customer.

How do we do the same? There are three specific things we can do to empower our people.

Set a Clear Vision for the Organization

As a leader, it's important to show passion and personal commitment to the direction of the organization and the values that the company is built on. In the case of Southwest, they had a clear vision to be the most loved, most flown airline and to be completely dedicated to customer service. They deliver that with warmth, friendliness, and heart. They are very clear on their mission; as I mentioned, they have a heart painted on the belly of each of their aircraft! The decision the pilot made to hold the plane was at a cost because Southwest prides itself on saving millions of dollars a year from their efficient operations in turning their planes around fifteen to twenty minutes faster than their competition. A pilot holding a plane for twelve minutes costs money, but instead of punishment, Southwest's leaders and executives fully supported the pilot's empowered decision because of the importance and value they place on customer service. Their vision is crystal clear.

Recognize Their Efforts and Reward Successes

Everyone deserves to feel important and appreciated, and in the case of Southwest, the CEO sends out a weekly shout-out to praise employees who've gone above and beyond to provide excellent customer service. They highlight positive behaviors publicly through their recognition and reward programs. The Southwest pilot felt confident in his decision at the moment he made it and was ultimately praised for demonstrating compassion by putting a customer before a short-term trade-off. Southwest executives shared the story and showed how proud they were of this pilot. They recognized and rewarded the behavior they expected to see and reinforced what it looked like, how it was done, and the why behind it. If people feel appreciated for the part they play, as I'm sure the pilot did, they're much more likely to go the extra mile to live out what is expected of them versus being fearful in a command-and-control kind of environment.

Trust Your Employees

The third way to empower your people is simply to trust them. Trust that they have the right intentions, that they're going to make the right decisions. Give them the right tools and the training, hire them to have the passion for what your company is about, and you've done your part as a leader to create that trust and that environment. If you're going to truly empower your employees, set a clear direction and reward the values and behaviors you expect to see, but remember to trust your employees and set them free to do their jobs.

That Southwest pilot didn't have to check in with anyone or ask for forgiveness. He was presented with a situation, and it was up to him to make a decision. He just did the right thing, and the executives had his back without question.

If you're going to truly empower your employees, set a clear direction and reward the values and behaviors you expect to see.

CHAMPION YOUR PEOPLE

How do we help develop possibilities in others while we're championing them? It is all about developing a growth mind-set. You're championing them with the idea of building a growth mind-set and helping them become their best possible selves. When I think about this concept, it reminds me of the family-owned grocery chain in the Northeast called Wegmans. We didn't have Wegmans stores in the Southeast where I lived, and I don't know of them from personal experience, but I have heard stories about them and know that they are consistently on the list of the nation's best places to work. They've been on the list for as long as there's been a list and have received numerous employee-centric awards. There was talk about how

Wegmans saw their employees as being their "secret sauce" or "recipe for success."

What is so intriguing is that this multibillion-dollar private company with over forty thousand employees is set apart as the most financially successful grocery chain in the US. They are the most recognized and enviable when it comes to their emphasis on taking care of their people. One of their corporate beliefs is that they can only achieve their goals if they fulfill the needs of their people. They are a great example of a company that has been able to grow while treating their people well. This is a differentiator; they make a difference against their competition, especially in an industry and in a world where you hear more and more about employee benefits being taken away and healthcare costs rising. There's so much about the employee value proposition that has decreased over the years, but they've figured out how to grow and thrive while treating their people well. How did they do it?

Commit to Development

Leaders can demonstrate their commitment to development by taking an interest in and fostering and encouraging employees' personal and professional growth while helping them develop their skills; leaders should also tend to their morale and happiness, which will create a sense of goodwill and loyalty. In the case of Wegmans, a happy, knowledgeable, trained employee creates a better experience for the customer as well, and that's been a contributor to their growth. Wegmans spends more than $50 million a year on training and development, and they awarded $5 million this last year in employee tuition assistance. Wegmans was voted number three on *Fortune*'s 100 Best Companies to Work For (2019).

Wegmans doesn't just spend money on classroom training and development. They invest in sending their employees on trips all over the world to become experts on the products they sell. For example, they may send a fish department employee to Alaska to learn about the quality standards of the fish. They'll send the butcher who cuts the steaks to Montana to learn about where the beef comes from. A deli manager might visit multiple countries in Europe to learn about the different cheeses he sells. It's pretty exciting, and their commitment is deeply rooted. Yes, they spend a lot of money, but it's money well spent since it enriches the lives of the employees and adds to their knowledge, allowing them to do their best work.

Over half of Wegmans store managers started out working in their stores in high school or college as part-time cashiers and have completed their education with the company's scholarship programs. If you look at their employee population, you'll find over 90 percent of the people who work there started at entry-level positions, bagging groceries or working in customer service. Wegmans is a great example of commitment to development.

Take a Chance on Them

Great things can happen when you are uncomfortable. Leaders who take a chance on their people and stretch them outside their comfort zones are inspiring creativity and learning. Such leaders are giving them new opportunities through projects or new responsibilities, but you must be there to catch them if they fall. Give them credit where credit's due but allow them the opportunity to make mistakes. This helps build trust and their confidence, allowing them to become better versions of themselves. Taking chances on them creates:

- loyalty,

- higher productivity, and

- effectiveness for the organization.

It's a win-win-win formula. Wegmans takes chances on their people. While developing a leader, they get that person ready for their next role, focusing on personal values and helping them examine what gives them happiness and fulfillment. It's a strength-based approach. Rather than firing somebody as a last resort, they work to match the strengths of the individuals and their desires. They use what gives a person happiness to match them to the right role.

A Wegmans employee ended up running the bakery in a store simply because the store manager loved her homemade cookies. This woman would bring the cookies in and share them with the store manager, and eventually they offered her the opportunity to manage the bakery. She took it, and now she can bake whatever she wants. That's an example of a company taking a chance on someone and having it turn out to be a success. However, if they take a chance and someone doesn't succeed, the company is there to catch them and then put them someplace where they can thrive; Wegmans will put them in a new position that gives them energy and allows them to be successful.

Inspire Better Performance

The third way to champion your people is to create opportunities for them to do better, to feel accomplished, and to shine. Leaders set the pace through the expectations and examples that they set. A leader can champion their teams or employees by reviewing their progress and driving accountability so the worker will step up their game and focus on continuous improvement. Once you develop your team, it's time to champion them to better performance. This is all about setting proper expectations so they reach their full potential and experience growth in their jobs and in their personal and professional lives.

Thinking back to Wegmans, we see that their commitment to their values is so strong that those values act as a guiding principle for the performance and excellence of the employees. They have this unspoken accountability to develop those around them because their values are so embedded. By creating an employee-centric company and putting so much energy into developing their people, they expect their employees to turn around and develop the people around them. They expect their people to continue to develop themselves and others, and this is done by telling stories and sharing experiences. It's this defined culture that has a measurable impact on the overall performance of the team. The mind-set says, "When you work for the best company, you're inspired to do your best work and be the best version of yourself. You're inspired to excellence."

LEARN FROM YOUR PEOPLE

A lot can be learned from the people you employ and the people you work with. Taking the time to extract experiences and tap into the passions and perspectives of others, you'll find that while you're doing this, you're modeling an open, transparent, curious, humble approach to your leadership. Learning from your people helps them build confidence in their own voices and their contributions. This is important for them on their paths to discovering what's possible in their own lives.

Every person you encounter has a catalog of experiences and knowledge, and by tapping into those resources, there's the possibility for exponential growth for you as a leader both for your business goals and the betterment of those individuals. Tapping into the experiences of others not only allows you to learn from them but also helps others formulate their values and their voices.

The Coca-Cola Company is another organization that is intriguing. Although I'm not a huge consumer of their products, I am enamored by them and have heard a lot about them over the years. A very successful global company, they have a mission to create moments of optimism and happiness in order to make a difference in the world. Over the years, my curiosity about the company has led me to ask some of our Coca-Cola clients about their organization. They would talk about the values of Coca-Cola and how the company has pledged to shape a better future and is committed to hearts and minds, wanting collaboration in what they do.

Last year, Coca-Cola announced their "World Without Waste" vision, and the company's goal is to have 100 percent collection and recycling by the year 2030. They want to collect and recycle a bottle or can for every single one they sell. When they announced this vision as an initiative, they had to admit that they were part of the problem because the litter created by their product is harming the planet. They had to accept the responsibility with a little humility and start modeling behaviors that are required to make a difference. They had to stop and say, "I'm going to take a moment to admit I'm part of the problem and recognize what's going on in the world around me," and learn from that.

Embracing a learning mind-set, they became willing to engage with more people and partners to hear new perspectives and accomplish their mission, which is much bigger than just one company, much bigger than Coca-Cola. How did they become inclusive and willing to engage with others so they could gain insights and outside perspectives to solve the problem? How do they continue learning from those around them?

Listen

The first way is to listen. It's all about fostering open communication, having a genuine interest in the points of view of others, and being curious. So many people talk about their understanding of the value of learning from others and their commitment to taking the necessary steps to do it, but then when they sit down with another person, they aren't really listening. This is a half-hearted attempt to learn. The beauty of learning from others comes from being open and willing to listen, from drawing someone in, which results in new opportunities for growth for both of us.

The beauty of learning from others comes from being open and willing to listen.

The "World Without Waste" initiative came about after the company listened to those who care about the planet, both their consumers around the world and their own employees. They listened intently, looking not just for feedback but for understanding of just what the people were saying. People were saying, "This is a problem. We care about the planet," and employees were saying, "We want to be proud of where we work" and "Hey, we're an industry leader with a deeply recognized brand, so we expect that you'll lead the way in this."

It wasn't enough just to listen to the feedback. Coca-Cola had to listen to people's ideas, feel what their intent was, and understand what they were trying to convey. After internalizing people's thoughts and concerns, they had to mobilize and implement what they heard. And that's just what they did. After listening to feedback and truly understanding the intent they'd gleaned from it, Coca-Cola brought thirty diverse employees together as a first step to develop the very specific goals for this mission. A team of employees did the research and made the recommendations, and the leadership listened to their ideas and made a commitment to implement them.

Collaborate

Creating opportunities for conversation and encouraging collaboration is a very effective way to learn from your people. From a leadership perspective, we may feel like we're communicating ("Oh yeah! I communicate all the time!"), but a lot of this goes one way and top down. Collaboration and communication need to be two-way streets. They provide opportunities to ask clarifying questions and find connections and common ground that will advance learning overall.

Collaboration is a critical part of learning, and we see this in a recent trend called "social learning." At the root of social learning is collaboration, the idea that informal learning—quick moments where people connect to share experiences with and ask questions of each other—has value. Social learning helps people connect. It generates conversation and ultimately promotes autonomy and self-direction because there's no expectation around it. Creating a community around these forms of collaboration can increase problem-solving, connection, and engagement. It can help people become their personal best selves.

For Coca-Cola, the "World Without Waste" initiative is all about community, but it's also an example of collaboration. Upward of three thousand leaders and subject matter experts both from Coca-Cola and other businesses and communities have come together to discuss the vision, set the goals, and advance the cause and the learning. It's a true collaboration and a true community. Executives came together to move the initiative forward and announced that it would be a global summit. They were very clear on the four important questions that need to be asked to be able to tap into the right experience.

While Coca-Cola was the one to bring the aspiration and mission forward, their role was to listen and learn through this unprecedented collaboration. Think of all the start-ups in Silicon Valley who for years avoided collaboration because there was not a clear distinction between collaboration and consensus building. The thinking was "Oh, that's too much. It slows things down. We have to go fast!" Speed took precedence over this idea of go slow to go fast. You have to make a distinction between collaboration and consensus.

Commit to Diversity

Finally, a great way to learn from your people is to commit to diversity. Diversity encourages new perspectives and understanding about how others experience the world. It's been proven that a team that has different perspectives outperforms a team with a single perspective in problem-solving, predicting future possibilities, and innovation. Diversification is an enabler, and bringing in new perspectives, skills, mind-sets, and insights is essential in solving the complex, global, high-stakes problems that businesses face today.

Leaders who see the value of diversity and inclusion, who support it authentically and create the environment for learning, are the ones who really demonstrate what it means to commit to diversity.

Leaders who see the value of diversity and inclusion, who support it authentically and create the environment for learning, are the ones who really demonstrate what it means to commit to diversity.

It's not enough to just see it as a mandate or a number such as "I have to hit a certain number of a certain employee population." It's about building bridges and interconnection that allows people to innovate and bring creativity to their work. The "World Without Waste" initiative was such a large mission that it needed diversity to accomplish it. When Coca-Cola kicked this off in 2016, they engaged stakeholders across the world. They pitched their idea at the World Economic Forum, really put it out there, and they accepted that it is a worldwide problem and that the solution would span every single process, team, and country. They needed to take both a top-down and bottom-up approach.

The World Economic Forum is a place to learn from global leaders and representatives of the world, and Coca-Cola took it upon themselves to engage more localized country populations. They sent teams to Africa, Brazil, Mexico, and Western Europe to make sure everyone really understood the mission and what the initiative looked like in different parts of the world in order to address the challenges everywhere. If in one part of the world, they simply needed to educate people about what it means to recycle, then that's what they did. Such solutions could be found because diversity was represented among a committed team of people who truly understood what was needed for a particular group. For something this large to work, everyone has to be personally connected to the mission. Everyone has to see and be seen, to speak and be heard.

GIVE THEM A VOICE

As a leader, whether you are developing those young in their careers or helping accomplished professionals elevate their skills to the next level, helping them to be seen and heard, to have their own voice, will make them better and will make the company better. The investment you make in them—to empower them, champion them, and learn from them—will further connect them to the work of the organization and help them, as current and future leaders, see the possibilities that exist in themselves.

There is a lot to apply, but there are things you can do immediately to help them grow confidence in their own voices and create the opportunities for them to contribute experiences and perspectives that are uniquely theirs.

Whether you are making eye contact in the hall, saying hello in the elevator, or making one small gesture that makes them feel like they matter, take the time now to make one commitment that will ensure your employees are seen and heard.

- To create a culture of empowerment and pride with my people, I will

  _____.

- To champion them and enable a growth mind-set, I will

  _____.

- To demonstrate humility and a community of learning, I will

  _____.

CHAPTER 8

CAPTURE YOUR OWN VOICE

To be a legacy leader, it is important to capture your unique voice and then use it. Not long ago I was working with a woman who was a successful leader in an organization and had received praise for her team's work. She had built great relationships across the organization, communicated effectively, and mobilized her team to action.

Based on her contributions and successes, she had a seat at the leadership table. She saw herself as a strong leader among her peers, yet when she looked around, she realized that she didn't want to just be a good leader; she wanted to be a great leader. She was accepting of her leadership responsibility and wanted to be able to more intentionally leverage her leadership strengths. She wanted to explore what she uniquely had that others didn't, to find her leadership voice and use it to elevate her presence and ultimately be the best version of herself to do her best work. The problem was she didn't know how to go about finding her unique voice.

FINDING YOUR PERSONAL LEADERSHIP BRAND

As I work with successful leaders, I better understand the importance of "presence." I describe this as how you show up. Your presence as a leader, your values, and your beliefs ultimately can be described as your personal leadership brand. It requires the following:

- reflection,

- intention,

- time, and

- effort.

Reviewing that list highlights why there is probably such a lack of focus among leaders that I work with on their personal leadership brand. However, why is finding your personal leadership brand so important? Identifying, understanding, and leaning into your personal leadership brand is the critical component to effectively, authentically, and confidently lead your team and your organization in this complex and demanding world. Your personal leadership brand ultimately becomes a culmination of your track record and the results you have produced. It's about the value that you bring to the table, the passions and talents you exhibit every day.

Your personal leadership brand should also be reflective of the impact you want to be known for and the legacy you want to leave behind. It gives you the opportunity to authentically show up, accept the responsibility that you have as leader, and get the job done.

Remember, you're not a solo act as a leader.

Remember, you're not a solo act as a leader. The most effective and rewarding way for you to do your job is to show up as yourself, know your own unique voice, and set the tone that is aligned with your values and beliefs. Your brand helps you gain congruence with the values of the organization and build credibility and relatability, which are necessary to achieve success and leave a lasting mark on the people.

TAKE AUTHENTIC INVENTORY

There are several steps involved in getting to know who you are as a leader, and they require a bit of effort. Taking an authentic inventory can help you reflect on your experiences and understand how you're perceived. It can capture what makes you unique and pinpoint the impact and legacy you want to leave. The three essential steps in taking an authentic inventory are

- personal reflection,

- perception check, and

- leadership brand design.

Let's begin with **personal reflection**. One of the best gifts you can give yourself is time. For the first step in taking your authentic inventory, you need to take the time to reflect on your personal experiences, thoughts, and feelings across different areas of your career and your life. Believe me, it's a worthwhile investment of your time. Personal reflection helps deepen the knowledge you have of yourself by clarifying what really matters to you personally, by acknowledging what you've accomplished and when you've felt most satisfied in your career, and by identifying the characteristics you've honed and leveraged effortlessly over your career. This reflection is the first step in defining your personal leadership brand, and it's also what I like to think of as a "happy heart" exercise.

The second step to taking your authentic inventory is a **perception check**. We have all heard the saying, "Perception is reality to those who hold it," and this exercise is not meant to change the perception of others. It's about objectively flushing out perceptions that exist, challenging your own reality, and expanding the view of the world that you're living in as a leader and as an individual. Reviewing past feedback and asking questions about others' current perceptions of you is an important step in clarifying your personal leadership brand. It's about aligning what you believe your personal leadership brand to be with what others really think of you.

Finally, we come to the **leadership brand design**. Most companies have a defined brand, and it sends a message about and reflects what's unique for that business. When you see well-known brands from well-known companies, they describe what business they're in and why they exist. Similarly, as a leader, your leadership brand is a culmination of what leadership characteristics you embody and how they separate you from other leaders. They highlight what is authentically yours and what you have that others don't. Designing your leadership brand is the final step in taking your authentic inventory and developing your personal leadership brand.

By going through these three steps, you will come to understand

> *Developing your personal leadership brand helps you communicate the value you have in your current company and will allow you to demonstrate your value to a new company in the future.*

what makes you unique and differentiates you as a leader, and you will see what you have to offer that others don't. Developing your personal leadership brand helps you communicate the value you have in your current company and will allow you to demonstrate your value to a new company in the future. It helps you be authentic in how you show up as a leader, giving you focus and clearly identifying your leadership voice. This unique leadership voice transfers to any position or company as your career progresses.

DECIDE HOW YOU WILL LEAD OTHERS

The work involved in developing a personal leadership brand is an intentional step in deciding how you will lead others. Leaders who establish their brand and commit to continuously aligning themselves with it are better positioned to succeed and feel like they're living their personal leadership best. This process can be extremely rewarding on a personal level because it helps improve your satisfaction and can prepare you for the next role or opportunity you're offered. In the complex world we live in today, understanding your personal leadership brand allows you to come from a position of strength and helps you maximize your effectiveness as a leader.

After reading through the process involved in taking an authentic inventory to develop your personal leadership brand, you may be thinking it's a bit overwhelming, that there's so much to do. The right coach can help you challenge and explore more deeply the individualistic nature of your brand, but don't worry—you can do this exercise on your own. I've been through this exercise alone and have coached my clients on it as well. It is possible. Having been through the exercise both for myself and with my clients, I can share the importance of keeping a journal. The process helps you expand your learning, but it really calls for you to draw on prior experiences and reflect on how they shaped your leadership traits and behaviors. Having journal entries on hand allows you to see how you were thinking and feeling during different experiences, and this knowledge is invaluable.

If you haven't started journaling yet, start now. Even without a collection of journals, you can still effectively walk through this process of finding your personal leadership brand. Let's step through the exercise together.

PERSONAL LEADERSHIP BRAND

This exercise is designed to help you create an authentic inventory of who you are. These steps require some time and effort but can help you reflect on your experiences, understand how you are perceived, and capture what makes you unique. In completing this exercise, you will have enough information to develop a statement that is reflective of your personal leadership brand.

Personal Reflection

Complete the following tasks to identify your core values.

1. List the roles you have had during your career. Pick the top job where you feel you had the most impact and were the most satisfied. Jot down a short narrative explaining why this was a great role.

2. Think about your customers and your team. Where have you identified pain points and been able to

resolve them with a solution? List the strengths and characteristics you leveraged.

3. Think about a leader in your past whom you admired and who had a positive impact on you. What characteristics and behaviors did you value most?

Perception Check

1. Review your most recent performance appraisals and any 360 assessments you have done. Jot down any patterns or feedback themes—positive or negative—that are apparent.

2. Select three to five people that you can ask questions of and gain their perceptions about you. Select business relationships where each sees you through a different lens (e.g., as a supervisor, direct report, peer, or mentor). Select at least one personal relationship (e.g., family, friend, or neighbor). Questions to ask:

   a. What do you see as the two to three points of difference that best define me?

   b. What should I do more of?

   c. What should I do less of?

   d. Where are my blind spots?

Summarize

Reflecting on the information you identified in the personal reflection and perception check, summarize your unique strengths, identifiers, and differentiators. While you're making note of the areas that are ripe for development or in need of improvement, focus on the qualities that come naturally to you and reflect your true identity as a leader.

You will use these qualities to define your **personal leadership brand**.

Design Your Personal Leadership Brand Statement

Complete the personal leadership brand statement below. Your **personal leadership brand** is what separates you from other leaders and is what you authentically have that others don't.

Finally, let's complete your **personal leadership brand design**. It's time to pull together all the information you summarized: the strengths, the unique identifiers, and the differentiators for you as a leader. Here's the statement framework:

As a leader, I am known for / committed to:

_____

so that

_____ .

It's your job to fill in the blanks, thereby creating your personal leadership brand statement. Once you've done this, ask yourself these questions:

- Does this reflect who I am?

- Does this describe my unique value creation as a leader?

- Is this the legacy leader I want to be?

Once you've given yourself the gift of time to truly reflect on and deepen your own learning of who you are and to take this authentic inventory, your personal leadership brand will emerge and you will have found your own voice. The benefits of finding your personal authentic voice are far reaching and will enable you to have the ability and confidence to relate to your organization and your team. It's important to remember that it isn't the point of arrival you're after here. This is a commitment to developing your personal best and therefore requires reflection, intention, time, and effort. I've found that leaders who go through this personal and professional exploration have been in a better position to be successful by leading with heart and leaving a legacy with their authentic and unique leadership brand.

CHAPTER 9

HOW TO BE A GREAT LEADER

Over the years, when I share with people that I have spent twenty-five years, my entire corporate career, with the same company, they give me a certain look and often ask, "How can that be? You look so young." Well, maybe they don't all question my age, but most people do find it quite unusual to be with the same company for such a long time. They begin a line of questioning around my role, responsibilities, or personality, assuming that I don't like change or was complacent in my role. They think I was content not to have anything new or stimulating in my life. That certainly wasn't the case, but it isn't long before such people ask the same question that I have learned to accept: "Well, what kept you there that long?"

My first response has always been, "The people. I loved the people I worked with because they were so committed to doing the right thing." Even if we were not always on the same page, we rallied around and supported each other when it mattered most. We truly cared about each other, and that is the main reason it was so hard to leave. With that said, the reason that made me want to stay was the opportunity to consistently, year after year and month after month, learn something new. It never felt like the same company because I was open to new opportunities and was curious.

My title, position, and ego never grew too big to learn, ask questions, and be curious even when I moved up in the organization to higher ranks, was relied on as a subject matter expert, and led a team or function. This growth mind-set is what helped me to be inspired and energized throughout my twenty-five-year career at the same company.

When it comes to this whole idea of great leadership, you need to ask the question, Are you learning as fast as the world is changing? In today's world, learning as fast as the world is changing is so critical to success for a couple of reasons.

EMBRACE CHANGE

Companies are striving for relevance and a competitive advantage. Every company must stay relevant, and the competition is so fierce in this regard. The speed of change in every industry is intense. The influence of digital requires that employees keep up in skills, knowledge, and abilities so that companies can stay relevant and outsmart the competition. You need to be able to problem solve with better ideas that have a cutting-edge perspective. That's one reason why continuing to learn is so important for companies.

The other reason is innovation and growth. A continuous-learning mind-set, the natural curiosity to ask questions, explore new ideas, and take risks, is what fosters innovation and new ideas for growth. Innovation requires curiosity, and companies appreciate risk-taking and curiosity. This whole idea of fail and learn, fail and learn, fail and learn is valuable work. This is why it's so important to continue to learn as fast as the world is changing.

However, even more than that, a growth mind-set and the commitment to continuous learning for individuals and leaders help to really open up your own personal feelings of satisfaction. The investments you make in learning keep you feeling personally inspired and enriched in your career and your life. For leaders, one way to combat this overwhelming, always-on nature of work today is through being a continuous learner.

I had a client who had been at the same company for over thirty years, and I was brought in as a coach for him. He was highly valued in the organization for his knowledge of the business and his relationships, calm demeanor, and ability to solve problems, but he

> *The investments you make in learning keep you feeling personally inspired and enriched in your career and your life.*

had fallen into a rut and started to develop behaviors that weren't reflective of a senior leader. He had low energy, was very impatient with his staff and peers, and was not motivating or motivated; some would describe him as grumpy. These behaviors had also started to spill over into his personal life at home. Not only was his boss noticing the impacts, but he himself was feeling the impacts.

By the time I started working with him, he had started to give up and was really feeling like his only option was to leave. He said to me, "I need to just leave this company. I've been at it for so long, and I need to start fresh. Clearly, it's the environment, and I need out."

Digging further, I learned that he had spent a good part of his career focusing internally on the business and on his team. For example, he hadn't picked up a book in over twenty years. He didn't make any time to attend conferences to learn new things. He even viewed off-site team meetings that were being set up by his leaders as bothersome or as an annoyance rather than an opportunity to learn and build up his energy and expand his thinking.

The demands of the job were getting to him. The speed of change—that always-on feeling and the reality of increasing customer expectations—all of that had really swallowed him up. He had forgotten how to learn. This is the exact scenario when a mind-set of learning and curiosity would be so impactful in combating these feelings. It was time for him to recrank the engine. The engine of learning.

We started with really small strategies. I recommended a couple books to him and an audio app where he could download book summaries that captured key ideas in fifteen minutes. I told him, "On your way into work, pull up this app and listen to a book summary." He started scheduling lunch with some of his peers who were fairly new to the organization and had come from other industries. We identified two conferences for him to attend within the next twelve months that sparked his interest. Through this process, I was able to help him create awareness of the importance of a growth mind-set and a learning mind-set.

These small steps helped breathe life and color back into him, back into how he was feeling as a valued leader for this organization. He found that these things gave him energy, and after a long day of being drained with problems and decisions, he was able to build his confidence. He found ways to share that information with others. It broke the monotony of the way he was approaching his days, and those simple changes helped him become a more confident senior leader who was now inspired and inspiring.

LEARN NEW SKILLS

Continuous learning and a growth mind-set are not as much of a problem earlier in your career. If you think about it, the younger you are in your career, or if you're just starting out, the more acceptable it is for you to be learning new skills with resources that are available, fresh, and new. If you're young in your career, not far in the distant past, you were maybe going through college or learning at your new job in a training program. The practice of learning isn't so far in your past when you're younger in your career.

Especially now, if we think about millennials who are young in their careers, we recognize that digital access makes information so accessible. Everything is available very easily. It's at our fingertips, and if you think about it, the term *google* has actually become a verb: "Google that." It's so easy and so normal to go after information and learn something new. This whole idea of lifelong learning has never been so important as the world embraces technology and the power of connection.

As you progress in your career, one of the best things that you could do for yourself is deliberately remember the feeling of seeking knowledge. What did it feel like when you were learning? If you can remember that feeling, it can help you combat what happens with time. Often, as you get older and advance further in your career, you become less comfortable in learning. Not knowing something and asking a question or being curious requires you to be brave. And that feeling of excitement from learning something new or from applying new skills and thinking in your role turns into a feeling of embarrassment or weakness as you progress in your career. There's this perceived expectation that you know all the answers because you're the boss. You get to a certain point when you think, "There's no need to keep learning" because now you've learned everything.

This reality kills our curiosity. As humans, if we don't know something and don't ask about it, what do we do? We tend to fill the void with assumptions. And assumptions are so dangerous for everyone, especially in this day and age. Assumptions are where judgment and poor decisions exist. If we aren't being curious and asking questions, we are prone to these things that aren't a good look for us as a leader. Killing our curiosity dulls the excitement of how we experience life and work, closing us off to new learning and new possibilities. It limits our opportunities to be our best selves.

Imagine if instead of pushing to answer a question or being saddled with an expectation that you know it all, you took the time to really indulge your curiosity and explored what was happening in the moment. Ask questions to learn and explore what might be possible. If you followed the ideas that are coming up for you and took it all in, how much more vibrant would your workplace be? The role of a leader isn't to know it all. The role of a leader is to imagine more and be curious in order to imagine more.

BE A SUCCESSFUL LEARNER

Over the years, I have developed two fundamental beliefs about how I would define a successful learner.

- Belief number one is that learners are not loners. The most powerful learning comes from unexpected places and requires humility. It requires humility to learn from everyone you encounter.

- Belief number two is learners model the way. Leaders aren't just learning for themselves; they're really setting the tone and modeling the behavior for those who are following them.

A leader as a learner is growing and developing their team and their organization as well as themselves. These beliefs and that thought process have helped provide the context, at least for me, in my journey. By being committed to a learning mind-set, I was committed to being a better leader.

These beliefs supported my two primary reasons for learning: learn for your own self-development so that you can continue to improve your job skills and leadership capabilities and learn for your organization or your team so that you can continue to add value and advance the goals of the organization forward. Here you will learn why these two primary reasons for learning are so important.

> *Leaders aren't just learning for themselves, they're really setting the tone and modeling the behavior for those who are following them.*

Learning for Yourself

The benefits of learning for your own sake are many. Learning can support you in improving areas of development. It can help prepare you to perform a new skill or develop the knowledge needed for a new role. It can also help you stay relevant, personally, in an industry that's continuing to change. It can make sure you stay open to possibilities so you can give even more of yourself. It can help you find new ideas and new ways for managing home and work, allowing you to bring your personal best every day. Learning for self-development might cover all those things, but whatever the reason for doing it, the outcome of learning for yourself is confidence, credibility, and satisfaction in your work and your home life.

Learning for Your Organization

Learning for your organization or your team can help solve complex problems or teach others something new. It can add new skills and capabilities that are needed for continuing the growth of the organization and the team. It can help bring new thinking to the table, challenge the status quo, and inspire excellence. Whatever the reasons, the outcome of learning for your organization and your team is that you have a better work product, and there's energy given to others in sharing knowledge and advancing their growth and development.

Whether you are keeping up with new tools or terminology in your industry, preparing yourself for life changes, taking the next step in your career, looking to achieve peak performance in your discipline, or simply setting new goals for your own personal and professional development, ultimately, the best leaders embrace a learning mind-set.

RECRANK THE ENGINE

How do you embrace a learning mind-set and recrank the engine? In my career I have experienced five specific ways that have all individually helped me and my clients maintain a growth mind-set and provide unique benefits personally and professionally. They include the following activities:

1. **Reading, podcasts, and audiobooks** help you to acquire new information. They force you to decipher and contextualize the information that you're getting through reading or listening. Ultimately, this learning helps improve your judgment and your decision-making.

2. **Mentoring** provides different perspectives and gives you a sounding board for a variety of topics. Working with a mentor can help you develop key business skills and provides a safe place to ask for advice and feedback.

3. **Networking** allows for the sharing and exchange of great ideas. The actual act of networking or making connections helps you understand more deeply the power of relationships and communication. As you become more visible through networking, new opportunities will present themselves.

4. **Formal and informal training** supports skill-specific development and also collaboration skills with your coworkers or with other people in the industry. Training helps you maintain your own competitive advantage by learning new skills. It also provides personal motivation that creates a positive feeling of progression.

5. **Coaching** can really advance awareness and development. Having a formal engagement with a coach or an accountability partner provides access to tools and assessments as well as one-on-one time that helps foster your own individual performance. Working with a coach advances your awareness and supports the development and achievement of your full potential.

Using these five areas interchangeably, you will discover there is no end to what you can learn and how far you can progress in being your personal leadership best. In a world that never stops

In a world that never stops changing, the best leaders never stop learning.

changing, the best leaders never stop learning. That is something that has always resonated with me. If you were to define an exceptional leader, you might characterize them as a great communicator. They are results oriented and command a room. They are respected and have a strategic vision for the company. If you were to look at any exceptional leader with those characteristics, you'd find they've only become proficient, mastered those skills, and been good in those roles because they were willing to learn, grow, improve, and change. Continuous learning is ultimately a critical component to success. Every job can be a classroom you never have to graduate from.

CHAPTER 10

REDEFINE SUCCESS

"How do you define success now?" I asked my client. I let the seconds on the clock tick away, giving her the space and silence needed to really reflect on her answer. It was an important and powerful question because this client had gone through a recent change in her career and was now questioning her decision. There was an expected learning curve in starting her own business, but things were taking longer than expected, and she was second-guessing the decision she had made and the passion that had originally given her the courage to take this step.

Before her decision to make a change, she was a very successful executive in the banking industry. To say she worked hard to get to the top of the male-dominated, old-school industry was an understatement. She had achieved success, with a big title, large team, and corner office, and was invited to all the strategy meetings where important decisions were made about the bank. She was being recognized and rewarded for her contributions, yet there was something missing. The job was taking more and more energy while providing less satisfaction to her personally than ever before. All of this was leading to a feeling that there was something more important out there and a chance to contribute in a way that had more meaning and purpose.

Most people never have the courage to leave the security and stability of an executive banking job for the chance to start their own business, but she did just that. It took months of us working together, but she overcame the insecurities, uncertainties, and fears. Fear of the unknown. Fear of failure. Fear of rejection. Fear of making the wrong decision. She was leaving what was familiar to embark on something unknown and unproven. She asked me, "What if I am not good enough?"

I told her, "There is no doubt in my mind that you can build new skills and master a new role. With your accomplished background and proven experience, what would make you believe you aren't good enough?"

"What if they don't like me?" she asked.

"Making this change is a bold decision, and it is normal to feel uncomfortable. You have expressed your passion in getting out there to build new relationships and networks. What makes you think you can't do it?" I asked in challenge.

Even though 60 percent of people want to make a career change, 94 percent let fear and uncertainty hold them back, and despite their desire, they never follow through with the decision to make a switch.[2] However, she did it and became one of the estimated 6 percent who make a career change to follow their passion on a new path. She had

---

2   "University of Phoenix Study Shows Majority of American Workforce Is Interested in Changing Careers but Worry About Risks of Starting Over," UOPX News, accessed August 13, 2019, https://www.phoenix.edu/news/releases/2017/07/sobus-career-change-survey.html.

made the decision to leave, did the work to reflect on what made her happiest, and set her sights and goals on her own business.

Months after she made that brave decision to launch her business, she was now free to focus on sharing her talents with the world. Starting your own business is hard. Pursuing your dreams is hard. What isn't so hard is getting distracted, falling back into comfortable habits, and taking the easy path. I remembered when an accomplished friend told me once, "Success comes effortlessly to someone who has already had it. Once you have been there, you know the path, and it's easy to do it again." In this case, my client was trying to find success following a new path. Clearing and paving a new road to success is anything but easy. Like with any journey, you need to have a clear picture of your destination. What does it look like?

Clearing and paving a new road to success is anything but easy. Like with any journey, you need to have a clear picture of your destination. What does it look like?

I asked her again, "How do you define success now?"

She answered by saying, "I receive positive feedback from my customers, as I am able to help them solve their problems. Now I have the mental energy to nurture the important friendships in my life, plus my new business affords me the opportunity to take time off during the summer to be with my kids. I also have a personal brand that feels authentic and allows me to be my best self every day."

"Okay," I replied. "So success now isn't your title, the size of your team, or your paycheck."

The work to be done from that moment was clear. I went on to say, "You need to leave behind any expectations associated with what was your vision of success and clarify your new vision of what it is and what it will be."

At such an early age, when opinions of what you should be and what path you should follow start to be defined, expectations are evident and success is defined by people around you. As a kid, if you are good at math, your parents may start to push you toward accounting. Or if you like to build things and tinker, you could be an engineer. As a parent myself, I continue to fight against the same thing, as I have a strong desire to project my own expectations on my high-school-age son. I just want him to be successful. The hardest thing to do is to back off and provide the guidance and direction he needs so he can explore his own path in life. It isn't about me and how I define success.

I have seen too many clients follow the path expected of them as young adults and continue on into their midcareers only to wake up one day realizing something is missing, feeling like there's something else out there and more important ways to contribute. We define success by our own measures. We are on our own journey, and most of the time where you think you will be isn't where you end up. For this client, as an example, and so many of us out there, it is time for an intentional reset. Redefining success is important; otherwise, you're not going to feel successful in your journey.

Redefining success is important; otherwise, you're not going to feel successful in your journey.

Making a large career transition can be frustrating, especially if you haven't taken the time to reset success. Defining the large goal and what you are driving toward long term but also setting small goals that are bite-size will help you acknowledge and celebrate the progress along the way. Many of my clients have a habit of "but whining" syndrome:

- "I launched my website, but I don't have many visitors."

- "I wrote an article on my expert topic, but it hasn't gotten enough attention."

- "I met with five new prospects this week, but I haven't closed any business."

This *but* whining minimizes the progress they did make and interferes with their ability to see success and just how far they have come against their goal. Personally, I can relate to these struggles. My personal health scare started me on my journey to live my best life. I left corporate America to start my own business. Before that, I was like many of my clients, spending years advancing my career and climbing the corporate ladder. Success measures were clear: the title, salary, size of my team, and so on. I worked endless hours and dedicated myself to focusing on business results, developing my skills and those of my team, and positioning myself to take on more responsibility. When everything fell into place, the measures of success showed themselves with my promotion to the large corner office.

Success wasn't something I thought about until I left that world and started my own business. My brave decision to follow my passion put me on the path of change where I was spending time honing new skills, forging new relationships, setting goals, crafting my elevator pitch, and planning my activities to set my business up for success. A lot of time was spent thinking about it, writing it down, talking about it. There were good days and bad days, then more bad days, not because I didn't love the work but because I wasn't feeling successful. Waking up with anxious feelings made me feel like I wasn't doing or contributing enough.

That first year I learned quite a bit and the most important aha moment for me was the fact that I was holding myself accountable to old measures of success. The ones from my prior life didn't align with the new life I had chosen for myself and my business. The realization hit me that I was the only one who could redefine what success looked like for my new life.

Your definition of success can and should change over time. When I took a breath, it gave me an opportunity to redefine my success measures intentionally. Redefining success measures as you move through life is important for the following reasons:

- It grounds you when you have bad days.

- It supports a sustained belief in yourself.

- It reminds you of your vision for yourself that is sacred and real even when you forget yourself.

For all of us, our identity and belief in ourselves shouldn't be wrapped up in our environment—what others want for us or what others perceive as success. Instead, our identity and belief in ourselves should lie in the vision of success we define for ourselves. Ultimately, they come through in our actions, mind-set, and relationships. They are present in the leadership we exemplify.

Actions: Are you engaged in activities that are congruent with your values, aligned with your passion, and energize you each day?

Mind-set: Are you focused forward while taking the time to reflect and acknowledge the small wins and all the things you are doing well?

Relationships: Are you supporting others in their success and making connections that advance overall learning and progress toward your potential?

For those of you who have already chosen courage over comfort and made the decision to follow a new path for yourself, there are two important questions that you need to answer and that will help you redefine success for yourself.

- Who do you want to be every day when you wake up?

- How do you want to contribute?

Contemplating these questions will give you greater insights into what is important—how you move through this journey and what matters most in your success.

THE FIRST STEPS TOWARD CHANGE

So many people don't have the mental energy to think about what needs to be done and the steps that need to be taken to embrace change, let alone the motivation to act on them. A great coach can help you through the struggle, but these strategies can help you take the first steps.

Step 1: Find the Capacity

Give yourself the space to let in new thinking. Think about those areas of your life that are draining your mental real estate. What worries or negative thoughts zap your mental energy? If you cleared them out, would it create the room you need to make a change?

Ask yourself, What is the one thing that needs to be considered or resolved for me to progress? Clear this hurdle, and move on to the next step. You aren't eradicating your fears but lessening the amount of room you give them in your life.

Step 2: Define Who You Want to Be

Get in tune with who you are when you are happiest and most fulfilled. More times than not, we focus on what we need to improve or develop. Think about a time when you were operating at your best. What strengths and characteristics did you leverage effortlessly?

Ask yourself, What characteristics do I value, and how do I want to contribute? This personal self-reflection deepens your individual learning by acknowledging when you have felt most satisfied and clarifying what really matters to you personally. This helps you come from a position of strength, which is especially important when facing the fears associated with making changes.

Step 3: Act

Now that you have had time to reflect inward and have a better sense of who you are and what you want, it is time to act. This doesn't mean it is time to walk into your boss's office and quit your job. Maybe for some this is an option, but more likely, it is an opportunity to use your downtime at work wisely and start your side hustle or a new job search.

Ask yourself, What do I need to do as part of the preparation for making changes? List these things, and start acting on them. This work demonstrates your readiness for the change you want to make and allows you to combat your fears by achieving small milestones toward your goal.

Embrace Fear

While fear can be paralyzing, it can also be the necessary catalyst for change. Learning to manage it includes facing your fear, understanding your fear, and being more intentional and planful in coming up with your strategy to overcome your fear. Fear can create productive discomfort, which in turn causes self-reflection and advances the learning and action needed to make changes in your life and career. It is possible to face your fears and push yourself out of your comfort zone. Making changes with these small steps can help you find the meaning and happiness in your life and the career that you deserve.

FINAL THOUGHTS

There is great irony in the fact that the very thing that set me on my journey—to leave corporate America, become a leadership coach, and write a book so that I could share my experiences and lessons with those leaders wanting to achieve their greatest potential—was a health scare. And more specifically, open-heart surgery. My heart as a leader—what led me to lead with care and compassion and the differentiator in what was described as the legacy I left behind at the same company after twenty-five years—would also be the specific issue that caused me to make intentional, significant changes and define new possibilities for my own life.

My hope is that it doesn't take something so drastic for you to realize your own true leadership potential. Do I want you to be encouraged to find more inspiration and meaning in your work? Yes.

In this book, I have shared many things that can help you

Do I want you to be encouraged to find more inspiration and meaning in your work? Yes.

lead with heart and leave a legacy in your leadership for all the right reasons. This labor of love is designed to inspire your actions and mind-set so you can genuinely and authentically live out your personal best leadership. You learned ways to be more

- engaged,

- self-reflective,

- authentic,

- empowering,

- collaborative, and

- inspirational.

At the end of the day, these examples all include characteristics and behaviors that can help you become an intentional leader—one who has presence and is present, one who leads with heart. If you take away one thing, I want you to leave knowing that what you accomplish as a leader is far less important than how you accomplish it. What's the best way to engage the hearts and minds of your people and create meaningful opportunities for them to do their best work? Be intentional in your how—how you show up, how you engage others, and how you lead.

Be intentional in your how—how you show up, how you engage others, and how you lead.

It was my heart surgery that helped me reflect so personally on what it means to be a leader with heart. The very thing that I placed so much intention on in my leadership role is what set me on a path to help others and what still inspires me today. You can be intentional and develop your own possibilities for yourself. You can define your own leadership legacy and build on a new world and new life. You can do it, and I would be happy to help. Are you ready for an incredible journey?

ABOUT THE AUTHOR

A student of human behavior most of her life, Tricia Manning watched her family dynamic change when her father was diagnosed with multiple sclerosis and couldn't work. Her mother became the breadwinner and full-time caregiver on a teacher's salary, motivating Tricia to find a part-time job in a continuing education program during high school. The program focused on leadership behaviors, competencies, and development that created an awareness within her at an early age about the importance of leadership.

Today, Tricia is a certified executive coach with twenty-five years in leadership positions, having reached the C-suite as only one of two female executives at the table. A highly regarded global practice leader with broad experiences in operations, strategic planning, and organizational effectiveness, Tricia has a strong passion for leadership development and gender diversity. She helps her clients explore ways to maximize their executive-level leadership skills and accelerate their overall professional development.

Her unique background allows her to bring real-life expertise and understanding around talent, culture, and leadership to every coaching engagement, and she is committed to helping individuals, teams, and organizations achieve positive results. Tricia believes this can be done with authenticity and by staying true to personal values, beliefs, and leadership styles.

Engaged and inspired by smart business leaders who manage it all personally and professionally, Tricia plays the role of coach, accountability partner, advisor, and consultant. Drawing on her experiences, skills, and *heart*, Tricia helps others elevate their leadership and develop new possibilities in how they show up and how they engage every day.

OUR SERVICES

Tricia is committed to coaching smart business leaders who manage it all personally and professionally so that they can elevate their leadership skills and develop new possibilities in how they lead.

Tricia understands what it takes to overcome so many of the challenges that successful leaders face today.

Does this sound like you?

- A leader who identifies as a legacy leader and wants to further leverage their authentic self to inspire excellence and drive positive outcomes in the business and the people.

- A minority leader who is committed to improving their own leadership effectiveness so they can excel as a member of a new and not-so-diverse leadership team.

- A leader who is facing a crisis—health, financial, or relationship—and is committed to making the personal and professional changes necessary to live their best life.

- A leader who feels stuck or no longer inspired by their work and needs support to make a change in mind-set and develop a plan of action.

- A leader committed to elevating their career and investing in the self-development necessary to achieve bold career goals.

As someone who has been through these challenges personally, Tricia specializes in helping her clients take the first steps necessary to create a life and career where they get to be their personal best every day.

One-on-one leadership coaching, high-performance team coaching, and custom session design and facilitation are just a few of the services that Tricia offers.

If you're interested in consulting with Tricia and learning more, please visit **triciamanning.com**.

The best, most impactful and memorable leaders are intentional in their HOW ... how they show up, how they engage and how they lead.

Having presence + Being present + Showing heart = Success

It is often showing heart—demonstrating real care and concern for people—that is the weakest link in the formula for most leaders.

What do you want to be known for? Do you want to leave a legacy behind?

Take the Heart Leader Assessment to find out.

Visit **http://triciamanning.com/lead-with-heart-and-leave-a-legacy-book/** to learn more about your HOW.